DON'T SWEAT
THE SMALL STUFF
AT WORK

DON'T SWEAT
THE SMALL STUFF
AT WORK

Simple Ways to Minimize Stress and Conflict

While Bringing Out the Best

in Yourself and Others

RICHARD CARLSON, PH.D.

New York

Library of Congress Cataloging-in-Publication Data
Carlson, Richard
Don't sweat the small stuff at work : simple ways to minimize
stress and conflict while bringing out the best in yourself
and others / Richard Carlson. — 1st ed.
p.   cm.
ISBN 0-7868-8336-7
1. Job stress.   2. Conflict management.   I. Title.
HF5548.85.C372   1998   98–41319
650.1'3—dc21   CIP

First Edition
10 9 8 7 6 5

Book Design by Jennifer Ann Daddio

This book is dedicated to you, my readers.
I hope it makes your life at work a little easier
and less stressful!

ACKNOWLEDGMENTS

I'd like to thank Bob Miller for his continued belief in my message and Leslie Wells who, once again, shared her insightful editorial skills with me. I'd also like to acknowledge the staff at Hyperion for their ongoing efforts. As always, I'd like to thank Patti Breitman and Linda Michaels for their enthusiasm, friendship and support. Finally, I'd like to thank my good friend Rhonda Hull for her assistance in keeping me focused and on-track while writing this book, and my incredible family who didn't "sweat the small stuff" while I was dedicated to this important project. Thank you all very much.

CONTENTS

DON'T SWEAT
THE SMALL STUFF
AT WORK

INTRODUCTION

Many of us spend an enormous amount of time and energy engaged in work—eight, ten, even twelve hours a day isn't at all uncommon. And whether we work for a giant corporation, a smaller company, or on Wall Street—or, whether we are self-employed, work for the government, or in retail—or for that matter any other industry or business, there's no doubt about it: Work can be, and usually is, stressful.

Each industry and career has its own unique set of problems and sources of stress, and each job carries its specific burdens and occasional nightmares. From time to time, most of us must deal with some combination of a variety of unpleasant issues—unrealistic deadlines and expectations, bureaucracies, difficult and demanding bosses, ridiculous meetings and memos, quotas, back-stabbing and criticism, harassment, uncertainty, and rejection. In addition, there are government regulations and high taxes, lack of appreciation, fierce competition, insensitive or selfish coworkers, demanding schedules, poor working conditions, long commutes, and downsizing. It seems that virtually no one is exempt from the hassles of having a job and doing business.

Indeed, the questions aren't whether or not stress exists in the workplace or whether or not you will be exposed to it—it most certainly does and you most certainly will. Rather, the more relevant question is, "How are you going to deal with it?" You can surrender to the fact that work is inherently stressful and there's nothing you can do about it, or you can begin to walk a slightly different path and learn to respond in new, more peaceful ways to the demands of work. It's clear to me that if you are going to find a way to work with less stress, you're going to have to find the answer within yourself. There simply isn't any job available, or any way to set up your life, that doesn't contain its own unique set of challenges.

If you've read any of my earlier books, you know that I'm an optimist. I believe that practically anyone can make at least incremental improvements in the quality of their lives by making small daily changes in attitude and behavior. Without minimizing any of the difficult issues that are out there, I know in my heart that we are not victims of the status quo. We *can* change. But change won't come about as a result of our work dishing out fewer demands or having an easier life. Rather, change must come from within us. The good news is, when it does, our work lives—in fact, our entire lives—will seem easier and less stressful.

This book came about as a result of thousands of letters and phone calls I received after writing *Don't Sweat the Small Stuff . . . And It's All Small Stuff.* Many people were pleased to discover that, after reading the book, their lives were becoming less stressful and more enjoyable. Time and time again, I received requests from readers to write a similar type of book, only this time focused on specific applications and issues in the workplace. Because, to a large extent, I have overcome my own tendency to sweat the small stuff at work and because I know many others who have done the same, I decided to embark on another *Don't Sweat the Small Stuff* journey geared toward work.

It's fascinating to examine the way people deal with the most serious work-related issues, such as being fired or overtaken by a larger competitor, internal theft or violence, or being forced to relocate to a new city. When you stop to think about it, it's quite impressive, if not amazing. For the most part, people are courageous, innovative, and resilient when forced to deal with these truly challenging problems. But, as in other areas of life, when dealing with the smaller daily "stuff," it's quite a different story. In fact, if you take a step back, you may realize that, despite the occasional significant problems in the workplace, much of what bugs us on a day-to-day basis is actually the "small stuff." Hopefully, for most of us, the truly serious and tragic issues are few and far between. Indeed, it's all those little hassles that tend to drive us crazy.

Imagine, for a moment, how much energy is expended being stressed-out, frustrated, and angry over relatively minor things. How about being offended and bothered, or feeling criticized? And think about the implications of worry, fear, and commiseration. What impact do these emotions have on our productivity and on our enjoyment of our work? It's exhausting just thinking about it! Now imagine what might happen if you could use that same energy—or even some of it—on being more productive, creative, and solution-oriented.

While there may be little we can do about the really "big stuff," you must admit that there are many instances when we blow little problems out of proportion and turn things into giant emergencies. Often, we become frustrated or overwhelmed by the accumulation of all the little things we have to deal with. So much so, that we begin to lump together the day-to-day hassles and begin to treat everything as if it were "big stuff."

Because there is so much "small stuff" to deal with at work, there is a correlation between the way you handle small stuff and the overall quality of your experience. There's no question that, if you can learn to treat the smaller hassles with more perspective, wisdom, patience and with a better sense of humor, you'll begin to bring out the best in yourself as well as in others. You'll spend far less time being bothered, annoyed, and frustrated, and more time being creative and productive. Solutions will seem as plentiful in a calmer state of mind as the problems appear in a more bothered state.

One of the nice by-products of learning not to sweat the small stuff so much is that, eventually, you begin to see more and more of what you have to deal with on a daily basis as "small stuff." Whereas before you may have treated practically everything as if it were a really big deal, you may get better at differentiating between the truly significant and that which is far more benign.

As you learn to stop sweating the small stuff at work, you'll still have many of the same problems to deal with. However, you'll experience them quite differently. Rather than reacting to each issue with knee-jerk negativity, you'll learn to respond with far more grace and ease. Your stress level will lower, and you'll begin to have a lot more fun. I know that work can be difficult, but I also know we can learn to respond to that difficulty in a more positive way. I wish you the very best of luck in your work life, and hope that this book makes it a little bit easier.

Let's go to it!

1.

DARE TO BE HAPPY

Many people don't allow themselves the luxury of being enthusiastic, light-hearted, inspired, relaxed, or happy—especially at work. To me, this is a very unfortunate form of self-denial. It seems that a great number of people are frightened at what a happy demeanor would look like to other people, including coworkers, clients, and employers. After all, they assume, "Someone who is relaxed (or happy) must not be a hard worker." The logic goes something like this: If they looked happy, others might assume they were satisfied with the status quo and therefore lacking the necessary motivation to excel in their work or go the extra mile. They certainly couldn't survive in a competitive environment.

I'm often hired to speak to corporations around the country on stress reduction and happier living. On a number of occasions, the person who invited me to speak has asked me, in a nervous tone, whether I would help the employees become so happy that they would "lose their edge." I'm not kidding!

In reality, it's the other way around. It's nonsense to believe that a relaxed, happy person necessarily lacks motivation. On the contrary, happy people are almost always the ones who love what they do. It's been shown again and again that people who love what they do are highly motivated by their own enthusiasm to continually better themselves and their performance. They are good listeners and have a sharp learning curve. In addition, happy workers are highly creative, charismatic, easy to be around, and good team players.

Unhappy people, on the other hand, are often held back by their own misery or stress, which distracts them from success. Rigid, stressed-out people are a drag to be around and difficult to work with. They are the ones who lack motivation because they are so consumed with their own problems, lack of time, and stress. Unhappy people often feel victimized by others and their working conditions. It's difficult for them to be solution-oriented because everything is seen as someone else's fault. In addition, they are usually poor team players because they are often self-centered and preoccupied with their own issues. They are defensive and, almost always, poor listeners. If they are successful, it's despite their unhappiness, not because of it. In fact, if an unhappy, stressed-out person can learn to become happier, he or she will become even more successful.

I felt this strategy would be an excellent way to introduce this book because one of my goals is to convince you that *it's okay to be happy, kind, patient, more relaxed and forgiving*. It's to your advantage, personally and professionally. You won't lose your edge, nor will you be "walked on." I can assure you that you won't become apathetic, uncaring or unmotivated. To the contrary, you'll feel more inspired, creative, and driven to make an even greater contribution than you do right now. You'll see solutions and opportunities where others see problems. Likewise, rather than being discouraged by setbacks or failures, you'll bounce back quickly and resiliently. You will have increased energy, you'll be able to work "in the eye of the storm," and, because you'll be so level-headed, you'll be the one who is looked to when tough decisions need to be made. You will rise to the top.

If you dare to be happy, your life will begin to change immediately. Your life and your work will take on greater significance and will be experienced as an extraordinary adventure. You'll be loved by others and, without a doubt, you'll be sweating the small stuff far less often at work.

2

BECOME LESS CONTROLLING

When I talk about being "controlling," I'm referring to unhealthy attempts to manipulate the behavior of others, having the need to control your environment, insisting on having things be "just so" in order to feel secure, and becoming immobilized, defensive or anxious when other people don't behave to your specifications—the way you think they should be. To be controlling means you are preoccupied with the actions of others and how those actions affect you. To put it in the context of this book, people who are controlling "sweat the behavior" of others when it doesn't match their own expectations.

I've made several observations about people who are controlling; two in particular. First, there are too many of them. For whatever reason, there seems to be a national trend toward controlling behavior. Secondly, the trait of being controlling is highly stressful—both to the controller and to those who are being controlled. If you want a more peaceful life, it's essential you become less controlling.

One of the most extreme examples of controlling behavior I've heard of involved, of all things, paper clips! A lawyer at a top-flight law firm had a penchant for certain things to be done in certain ways—not only "big picture" things, but very minuscule things as well. This fellow liked to use copper-colored paper clips instead of the silver ones his firm provided (what could be more important than that?). So he had his secretary buy his own private supply for him each week (and didn't even reimburse her). If something came to his desk with the wrong kind of clip, he'd fly into a rage. He became known in the office as "the paper clip king."

It probably won't come as a big surprise that this guy was almost always behind on his paperwork, and his work for his clients suffered. All the time he spent getting angry over petty things slowed him down. The paper clips were only one aspect of his controlling behavior—he had rules and regulations about everything from how his coffee was served (in a special china cup and saucer) to the order in which he was introduced in meetings. Ultimately, his controlling behavior turned off one too many of his clients, and he was let go from the firm.

This is a very unusual and extreme example, yet if you examine your own behavior, you may find areas that you are trying to control that are futile or just plain silly. I encourage you to take a look.

A person who is controlling carries with him a great deal of stress because, not only does he (or she) have to be concerned with his own choices and behavior, but in addition, he insists that others think and behave in certain ways as well. While occasionally we can influence another person, we certainly can't force him to be a certain way. To someone who is controlling, this is highly frustrating.

Obviously, in business, there are many times you want to have a meeting of the minds, or you need others to see things as you do. You have to sell yourself and your ideas to those you work with. In certain instances, you must exert your opinions, influence, even power to get something done. There are times you must insist on getting your way or think of clever and creative ways to get others to think differently. That's all part of business. And that's absolutely not what I'm referring to here.

We're not talking about healthy, normal attempts to come to a meeting of the minds or balancing points of view. We're also not talking about not caring about the behavior of others—of course you care. Rather, we're discussing the ways that insistence, singular thinking, rigidity, and the need to control translates into pain and stress.

What hurts the controlling person is what goes on inside—his feelings and emotions. The key element seems to be a lack of willingness to allow other people to fully be themselves, to give them space to be who they are, and to respect—really respect—the fact that people think differently. Deep down, a controlling person doesn't want other people to be themselves, but rather the image of who they want them to be. But people aren't an image of who we want them to be—they are who they are. So, if you're tied to an imagined image, you're going to feel frustrated and impotent a great deal of the time. A controlling person assumes that he knows what's best, and by golly, he's going to make other people see the folly of their ways. Within the need to control, there's an inherent lack of respect for the opinions and ways of others.

The only way to become less controlling is to see the advantages of doing so. You have to see that you can still get your way when it's necessary, yet you will be less personally invested. In other words, less will be riding on other people being, thinking, or behaving in a certain way. This will translate into a far less stressful way of being in the world. When you can make allowances in your mind for the fact that other people see life differently than you do, you'll experience far less internal struggle.

In addition, as you become less controlling, you'll be a lot easier to be around. You can probably guess that most people don't like to be controlled. It's a turnoff. It creates resentment and adversarial relationships.

As you let go of your need to be so controlling, people will be more inclined to help you; they will want to see you succeed. When people feel accepted for who they are rather than judged for who you think they should be, they will admire and respect you like never before.

3.

ELIMINATE THE
RAT RACE MENTALITY

I often hear people conversing about being stuck "in the rat race" as if they were discussing the weather—in a very casual, matter-of-fact manner. The assumption seems to be, "There's no escaping it—it's just a fact of life for everyone."

One of the problems with this mentality is that the label "rat race" implies, among other things, assumptions like, "I'm in a hurry, get out of my way, there's never enough time, there's not enough to go around, it's a dog-eat-dog world," and so forth. It sets you up to be frightened, impatient, and annoyed by constantly reinforcing and validating a self-defeating belief. You'll notice that most people who describe themselves as being "in the rat race" will indeed be hyper and easily bothered. It's important to note, however, that there are other people with the same types of jobs, pressures, responsibilities, and schedules who experience and describe their work in a much more peaceful and interesting way. Yet, they are every bit as effective and productive as their more nervous and agitated counterparts.

It's always refreshing for me to meet people who, despite being part of the corporate, commuting, and/or working world, have made the decision to not buy into this frenetic and destructive label. They refuse to box themselves in by the way they describe their experience. Instead, they live in a more accepting way, constantly on the lookout for a positive take on their experience.

So much of our daily work life exists in our own mind, dependent upon what aspects we focus on and how we characterize our experience. In other words, when we describe our day, we might feel very justified in saying, "Oh God, it was awful. I was stuck in horrible traffic with millions of other angry people. I spent my day in boring meetings, always scrambling a few minutes behind. There were arguments and almost constant conflict to deal with. What a bunch of jerks!"

The identical day might be thought of differently. You might describe it like this: "I drove to work and spent much of my day meeting with people. It was a challenge, but I did my best to stay as long as possible at one meeting without being late for the next one. The art of my work is bringing together people who, on the surface, don't seem to be able to get along very well. It's a good thing I'm there to help."

Can you feel the difference? And it's not a matter of one description being "realistic and accurate" and the other being wishful thinking. The truth is, both are absolutely accurate. It all depends on the well-being of the person doing the thinking. The same dynamic applies to whatever you happen to do for a living or how you spend your time. You can always make the argument, "I'm stuck in the rat race," or you can find another way to think about it.

You can begin to eliminate the rat race mentality and, in the process, become a calmer person and create a more interesting life, by deciding to stop discussing it with others—and by recharacterizing your day and your responsibilities in a healthier way. As your mind is focused in a more positive direction, and as you're looking for the gifts of your day instead of the hassles, you'll begin to notice aspects of your work life that may have been invisible to you. You'll actually see things differently. Everywhere you look, you'll see opportunities for personal and spiritual growth. You'll see more solutions and fewer problems, as well as plenty of ways to enhance and maximize your experience. I hope you'll consider eliminating the rate race mentality—your work will be a lot more rewarding if you do.

4.

DON'T DRAMATIZE
THE DEADLINES

Many of us work under the constant demands of tight deadlines. Authors are no exception to this rule. But have you ever stopped to think about how much mental and emotional emphasis we put on our deadlines? And have you ever wondered what negative consequences are attached to such emphasis? If not, I encourage you to give these questions some careful consideration.

It's true that deadlines are a fact of life. Yet a lot of this type of stress comes not so much from the deadline itself, but from all the thinking about it, wondering whether or not we will make it, feeling sorry for ourselves, complaining and, perhaps most of all, commiserating with others.

Recently, I was in an office waiting for an appointment. The person I was to meet with had been delayed in traffic. I was trying to read, but became fascinated by a conversation between two co-workers in the office. They were complaining among themselves about the unfair tight deadline they were on. Apparently, they had less than two hours to complete some type of report. Whatever it was, it was to be turned in by noon that same day.

I sat there, listening in amazement, as the two of them spent almost an entire hour complaining about how ridiculous it was to be put through this. They had not taken the first step toward the completion of their goal! Finally, about a minute before the person I was to meet finally arrived, one of them said in a frantic tone, "God, we'd better get started. It's due in an hour."

I realize that this is an extreme example, and few of us would waste time in as dramatic a manner as this. However, it does illustrate the point that the deadline itself isn't always the sole factor in the creation of stress. Ultimately, these two people seemed to realize that they could get the job done—even in one hour. So you have to wonder how different their experience could have been had they calmly taken a deep breath and worked together as quickly and efficiently as possible.

It's been my experience that complaining about deadlines—even if the complaints are justified—takes an enormous amount of mental energy and, more important to deadlines, time! The turmoil you go through commiserating with others or simply within your own head is rarely worth it. The added obsessive thinking about the deadline creates its own internal anxiety.

I know that deadlines can create quite a bit of stress and that sometimes it doesn't seem fair. However, working toward your goal without the interference of negative mental energy makes any job more manageable. See if you can notice how often you tend to worry, fret, or complain about deadlines. Then, try to catch yourself in the act of doing so. When you do, gently remind yourself that your energy would be better spent elsewhere. Who knows, perhaps you can ultimately make peace with deadlines altogether.

5.

HAVE SOME "NO PHONE"
TIME AT WORK

If you're like me, the telephone is a mixed bag of goods. On one hand, it's a lifesaver and obviously critical to most people. Without it, work would be impossible. On the other hand, depending on what you do for a living, the telephone can be one of the most distracting and stressful aspects of your work. Sometimes it seems as if we're always on the phone. And, if we're on the phone, it's impossible to get any other type of work done. This can create anxiety and resentment toward the people who are calling us.

I was once in the office of a manager when the phone rang. Immediately, he bellowed, "That darn phone never stops ringing." He then proceeded to pick it up and engage in a fifteen-minute conversation while I waited. When he finally hung up, he looked exhausted and frustrated. He apologized as the phone rang once again. He later confessed that he was having a great deal of trouble completing his tasks because of the volume of calls he was responding to. At some point I asked him, "Have you ever considered having a certain period of time when you simply don't answer the phone?" He looked at me with a puzzled look on his face and said, "As a matter of fact, no." It turned out that this simple suggestion helped him not only to relax, but to get more work done as well. Like many people, he didn't need hours of uninterrupted time, but he did need some! Because he was the one returning many of the calls instead of responding to them, he was able, in many instances, to cut the length of the return call. He would say things like, "Hi Joan, I've only got two minutes, but I wanted to get back to you."

Obviously, we depend on the phone, and are required to use it to varying degrees. If you're a receptionist, for example, or a telephone operator, or a salesperson, this strategy is going to have limited, if any practical relevance for you. However, for many others, it can be a real lifesaver. In my office, for example, if I didn't have any "no phone" time, I would be on the phone close to 100 percent of the day. The phone never seems to stop ringing. If I didn't have protective policies in place, I'd have very little time to write or work on other projects. I suspect the same may be true for many of you.

You can set this strategy in place in many different ways. I have certain times of the day when I turn off the ringer and don't take any calls other than ones that have been previously scheduled, or for real emergencies (which are extremely rare). This gives me some time to focus— without distraction—on what's most relevant to my work.

Many people, of course, are required to answer the phone as a company policy or as a part of their job, and these people must be a little more creative to implement this strategy. Perhaps you can arrive a little early and turn off the phone before your day "officially" begins, or do the same thing after work. I know one woman who decided to bring her lunch to work so that she could work at her desk during a time she was allowed to turn off the phone and let the voice mail answer it. She was able to negotiate an earlier quitting time so that her actual day wasn't longer, but she was then able to have a little more time to concentrate.

In certain instances, you might be able to convince your employer to allow you to experiment with this strategy—to see if you can get more done (and still return all the calls). Some calls that come in can be returned later, or after hours when you can answer specific questions by leaving messages on a voice mail. This may take a minute or two instead of engaging in a ten- or fifteen-minute conversation.

If you work at home (or if you ever need to get things done at home), this strategy works wonders and is often easier to put into place. You simply make the decision that for a specific period of time you will not answer the phone, thereby giving yourself the chance to get the things done that you need to do.

This is not a fool-proof strategy; there are often quirks to work out. For example, how do you handle emergencies or important personal calls? I have a separate line reserved for very close friends, family, and a select few people that I work with. Another possibility is to leave your pager number or an alternate phone number on your voice mail or answering machine that is specifically reserved for calls that truly can't wait. Most people will honor your "emergency only" request. One other possibility is that you can check your messages after each call, or on a frequent basis. That way, you can postpone the bulk of the calls until a better time, but still get right back to those people who absolutely can't wait.

I think you'll find that any hassles you must overcome to put this strategy into practice are, in most instances, well worth it. Let's face it. The work world is not going to accommodate us with fewer phone calls to respond to. I've found that I can get twice, even three times the amount of concentrated work done when I'm not distracted by the phone. Then, with all the time I have saved, I can almost always return my calls when everything else has been done.

AVOID CORPORATE BRAGGING

One of the many things that I do professionally is travel around the country giving lectures to corporations and other groups on stress reduction, gaining happiness, and various ways to stop sweating the small stuff. At some of these functions, I'm asked to attend meetings, meals, and parties, either before or after my speaking engagement. And although I'm a fairly private person who enjoys being alone, particularly before I speak to a large group, I'd say that a vast majority of the people I've met are nice, thoughtful, talented, and well-meaning individuals.

I've noticed a destructive tendency, however, that seems to run through virtually every individual, corporation, and industry. That tendency is what I call "corporate bragging."

Corporate bragging is sharing with others how incredibly busy you are and how very hard you work—not just in passing, but rather as a central, focal point of conversation. It's almost as though we wear a badge of honor for being a person who is completely overwhelmed, deprived of sleep, and who has little, if any, personal life. I've heard hundreds of people discussing the number of hours they work, as well as the number of hours they don't get to sleep each night. I've heard people explain how exhaustion is a regular part of their life. They discuss the time they arrive at the office, and the number of months it's been since they had any real quality time with their spouse, children, or significant other, much less a vacation. I've heard people brag about not having time to go out on dates, about being so busy and frantic that they've forgotten to eat, and even a few people who have gone so far as to say they rarely have time to use the restroom.

Although corporate bragging is a catchy phrase, the tendency itself is certainly not limited to people working in the corporate world. Rather, it's a habit that seems to have taken hold over most people who work for a living—it's extremely pervasive.

Before I go on, let me assure you that I'm not minimizing how hard people work or how difficult and all-consuming work can be—I've been there too. The problem is that bragging about how busy you are reinforces, to yourself, how stressed out you are. It keeps you overly focused on the most negative aspects of your work. It becomes a self-fulfilling prophecy, keeping you caught up in your own business.

If you take a step back and think about it, you'll probably agree that corporate bragging is also a boring, nonproductive topic of conversation. I've observed many conversations centered around corporate bragging and I've yet to see a single person even slightly interested in hearing about someone else's busyness. Usually, the person listening (if you can call it that) is either waiting their turn to share about their own busyness, or they are looking around the room, paying little attention to what is being said. The truth is, "busyness" is old news—everyone else is already talking about it.

Think about it from the perspective of those to whom you are sharing. Unless I'm missing something, regardless of who you are or what you do for a living, it's not very interesting to hear about how busy or overwhelmed you are. In fact, it's really boring. Personally, I can't stand listening to people complain about it—and I try really hard to avoid it. Let's be realistic. Would you be interested in hearing about how busy I am? I hope not. I'd rather be around people who discuss interesting aspects of life—and I'm sure you would too.

So, no matter how you look at it, corporate bragging does no good. If you're too busy, you either need to cut back, or catch up. But talking about it to others only exacerbates your stress and makes you a less interesting person.

7.

MAKE THE BEST OF
THOSE BORING MEETINGS

I did a fairly comprehensive survey asking people what they liked least about work. Over and over again, people shared with me their distaste for all those meetings, especially the "boring" ones. Many people feel there are simply too many meetings to attend on a daily and weekly basis, and that many of them are entirely unnecessary.

Admittedly, due to the nature of my work, I'm not required to attend as many meetings as some people. However, I have developed a strategy regarding meetings that has helped me a great deal. And those who have tried it have reported back a similar result.

I've found two secrets to making virtually any meeting interesting and as productive as it can possibly be. The first thing I do is use the meeting to practice being "present moment oriented." In other words, I attempt to absorb myself in the meeting—not allowing my mind to wander. This deliberate attempt to be focused allows me to get as much value out of the experience as possible. After all, I'm there anyway. I can spend the time wishing I were somewhere else—or I can think about what I'll be doing later. Or, I can practice being truly present, a really good listener. This helps me be highly responsive to whatever is being discussed. That way, if there is something I can contribute, I'll be able to do so.

Since I've been doing this, I've found that the meetings I attend are far more interesting. Additional insights come to mind, and I feel as though I have more to offer. I've also noticed an increased sense of respect from others. They may even not be consciously aware of it, but it seems that when those present in a meeting sense that you are truly listening, they want to listen to you as well. There is a powerful sense of well-deserved trust that comes across when you are truly present. People are drawn to your energy and presence.

The second commitment I have made regarding meetings is to tell myself that I'm going to learn something new from each meeting. So, I listen intently to what is being said, trying to hear something I don't already know. In other words, rather than comparing what I'm hearing to what I already believe—or agreeing or disagreeing in my mind to what is being said—I'm searching for new wisdom, a new insight, or a new way of doing something. I've found that when my intent is to learn, I almost always do learn. Instead of thinking to myself, "Yeah, yeah, I already know this stuff," I try to clear my mind and allow myself to have a beginner's mind.

The results have been quite impressive and significant. My learning curve has dramatically increased, and meetings have become fun again. I've learned to make the best of it. The way I look at it is this: I'm in the meeting anyway. Why not spend the time in a productive, healthy way, practicing valuable emotional skills instead of wishing I were someone else? To do so makes my work life more interesting and effective.

8.

STOP ANTICIPATING TIREDNESS

Recently, I was on a flight from San Francisco to Chicago when I over-heard one of the silliest conversations imaginable. It demonstrates a critical yet common mistake that many people seem to make on an ongo-ing basis. The conversation, which must have lasted at least half of an hour, centered around how tired each of these two people were going to be—tomorrow and all week!

It was as if each person was trying to convince the other, and perhaps themselves, how many hours and how hard they were working, how few hours of sleep they were going to get, and, most of all, how tired they were going to be. I wasn't quite sure if they were bragging or complain-ing, but one thing was certain, they were appearing more and more tired the longer the conversation continued.

They each said things like, "Boy, am I going to be tired tomorrow," "I don't know how I'm going to make it through the rest of the week," and "I'm only going to get three hours of sleep tonight." They told stories of late nights, lack of sleep, uncomfortable hotel beds, and early morning meetings. They anticipated feeling exhausted, and I'm sure they were going to be correct in their assumption. Their voices were heavy, as if the lack of sleep they were going to get was already affecting them. I actual-ly felt myself getting tired just listening to part of the conversation!

The problem with anticipating tiredness in this way, or in any way, is that it clearly reinforces the tiredness. It rivets your attention to the number of hours you are sleeping and how tired you are going to be. Then, when you wake up, you're likely do it again by reminding yourself how few hours it has been since your head hit the pillow. Who knows what really happens, but seems to me that anticipating tiredness must send a message to your brain *reminding* you to feel and act tired because that is the way you have programmed yourself to respond.

Clearly, everyone needs a certain degree of rest. I've read a few articles suggesting that many, if not most, of us don't get enough sleep. And if you're tired, the best possible solution would probably be to try to get more sleep. But in those instances when it's not possible to do so, the worst thing you can do, in my estimation, is to convince yourself, in advance, that you are going to be exhausted. I've found that the best strategy is to get as much sleep as I possibly can and be grateful for whatever amount that might be.

Because I travel a great deal for speaking engagements and promotional events, there are times when I get as few as three or four hours of sleep, occasionally even less. I have noticed, however, that if I simply forget about it—absolutely avoid the tendency to keep track—I'm far more rested with the sleep I do get. Then as soon as I can, I take a nap, and all is usually well. One thing I try never to do is to discuss my lack of sleep with other people. I've learned that when I do, I always feel more tired as a result.

I've noticed this habit of anticipating tiredness creep into the conversations of many people (don't feel bad, I've done it plenty of times in the past). If you are someone who does this, see if you can avoid the tendency as much as possible. If you do, you may find yourself feeling less tired. It seems reasonable to assume that, if you aren't as tired, you probably won't be sweating the small stuff as much at work.

9.

DON'T SWEAT
THE BUREAUCRACY

I can't imagine that there are very many people who work for a living who don't have to deal with at least some form of bureaucracy. After all, there are local, state, and federal agencies, insurance companies, Social Security, Medicare, the post office, the Department of Motor Vehicles, city hall, payroll procedures, business licenses, permits required, regulatory agencies, and, of course, the IRS—to name just a few. Most industries seem to have their own agencies to deal with—education, medical, pharmaceutical, food and beverage, the airlines and other forms of transportation, the building industry, the environment, and all the rest.

You can, of course, spend your entire lifetime complaining about bureaucracy, wishing it would disappear, and fighting every step of the way. You can struggle, engage in negative dialogue, play out wars in your head, and drive yourself crazy. In the end, however, you're still going to have to deal with bureaucracy. My suggestion is to stop sweating it and, in fact, strive to make peace with bureaucracy. This is something that can be done.

Joe has a small business with six employees. He received a notice from his state tax agency verifying the closing of his business. The problem was—it wasn't closed! When he would call or write to clear the matter up, he was told again and again that he must be mistaken—the business was officially closed. It took six months, but the problem was eventually resolved.

The key to the resolution of this issue was Joe's lack of panic. He told me, "Statistically, sooner or later something like this was bound to happen." Rather than panic or go crazy, he kept his cool and maintained his perspective.

Let me make myself perfectly clear. I'm not suggesting that you roll over and become a victim of bureaucracy—or that you think of being caught in ridiculous bureaucratic loops as acceptable. Nor am I suggesting that you smile when confronted with one of those "from a different planet" conclusions that some bureaucrats seem to come up with. What I *am* suggesting is that you find a way to maximize your efficiency when you must deal with bureaucracy, do the very best that you can with it, make suggestions on ways to improve the system, and then detach yourself from the craziness.

When dealing with bureaucracy, it's important to take this attitude: "I know there is a solution here and I know this will be resolved." There are certainly indescribable exceptions where there is such a mess that there doesn't seem to be a way out but, luckily, in a vast majority of the cases, a resolution is eventually achieved if you are patient, persistent and don't worry about it. Develop a sense of humor and, if possible, see if you can accept the fact that rules and regulations do have a place in our society. We have just allowed it to become a little out of control.

This past year I've been trapped in two unbelievable bureaucratic webs—one with the Department of Motor Vehicles and one with a city agency dealing with a home-related project. In both scenarios, for a brief period of time, logic and common sense were removed from the picture. I found myself wondering what planet I was on! Yet, to the best of my knowledge, both situations have resolved themselves.

There is a bright spot. There are people within the bureaucracy that don't fit the mold—people who are flexible and who are trying to be of service. When you must deal with bureaucracy, try to find these people—they are out there. In both of my recent adventures, I was helped by wonderful, caring people who stepped out of the mess long enough to help me. And you know what else? Most people who work for a bureaucracy are just as frustrated as you and I. For the most part, they are really nice people who are, to some degree, trapped in a role.

Keep in mind that people who work for the IRS have to pay taxes—and most people who work for the Department of Motor Vehicles probably drive a car. They are just like the rest of us; none are exempt from dealing with bureaucracy. So the lesson is this: The more you are able to keep your bearings and composure, and have some perspective, the more likely it is that you will find one of these nice people to help you. Getting frustrated only makes matters worse. It brings out the worst in bureaucrats and encourages them to turn to the rule book rather than find a real solution.

I know this is a tough issue—it is for me too. Yet our options aren't good. I've thought about this issue a great deal and have come to the conclusion that it's not worth it to become frustrated. Far better to stop sweating the bureaucracy.

10.

REMEMBER THE PHRASE, "BEING DEAD IS BAD FOR BUSINESS"

Several years ago my father was involved in a wonderful organization called BENZ, which stands for Business Executives for National Security. One of their missions was to educate business professionals about the absurdity of the nuclear arms race, both the financial burdens as well as the outright dangers to all of us. One of my favorite sayings that came out of BENZ was, "Being dead is bad for business." In a humorous way, they were emphasizing the obvious—if we blow ourselves up, none of us will prosper!

I'll bet you can guess where I'm going with this one. You can, of course, easily extend this clever metaphor to the way we treat ourselves—particularly in the areas of our personal health. The saying holds true however you look at it: Being dead is bad for business.

Remembering this really helps to keep things in perspective. For example, when you find yourself saying things like, "I don't have time to exercise," what you really should be saying is, "I don't have time *not* to exercise." If you lose your health and sense of well-being, you won't make it to work at all. In the long run, it takes far less time to take care of yourself than it does to lose your ability to function well.

Jim was a partner for a large New York law firm. Although he loved his family as much as anyone I've ever met, he was burning the candle at both ends. He left early and came home late. He traveled a great deal and was under constant stress. His children were growing up and he was missing most of it. He lacked sleep and exercise. He said to me, "Richard, this pace is going to kill me." To make matters worse, there didn't seem to be any light at the end of the tunnel. The more valuable he became to the firm, the more demands were made of his time.

At some point, it all became too much. After a great deal of personal reflection, he came to the conclusion that, as important as his work was to him, it wasn't worth dying for, nor was it worth missing the opportunity to watch his own children grow up. He decided a change was in order. He quit the firm and opened his own practice. I've never seen a more magnificent transformation. Not too long ago, he said to me, "I've never been happier. Business is better than ever and, for the first time, I'm able to spend a considerable amount of time with Julie and the kids." Although he still works very hard, he has created a sense of balance that works well for him. There's little question that, had he continued on his earlier path, his health and happiness would have continued to deteriorate. It seems that he literally decided that being dead would be bad for business!

Obviously, not everyone can make such a dramatic and risky change, but doesn't it make sense to eat well, exercise, get plenty of rest, think positively, have regular physical checkups, and partake in other healthy habits? In addition to the obvious problems associated with ignoring these commonsense health habits, you can see that it's also a horrible waste of time in the long run. Each cold or flu costs you days of productive work time. Who knows how many years of time you will save by simply taking care of yourself?

By remembering that "being dead is bad for business," you'll probably begin taking better care of yourself—physically and emotionally. You'll feel better, be happier, and probably live longer. You can let go of your fear that you'll fall behind because, in fact, you'll be more productive and have a longer, happier career. So keep yourself alive and healthy. It's good for business.

11.

MAKE THE BEST OF
CORPORATE TRAVEL

For many business professionals, mandatory travel is somewhat rare, if not nonexistent. Yet those of us who must travel, especially a great deal, know very well the hassles associated with frequent travel. Rushing around, delays and cancellations, long periods of time in closed-in spaces, never-ending impatient crowds, safety fears associated with flying, living out of suitcases, time-zone changes, sleep problems, hotel food, and many other factors, are simply a necessary evil.

There is probably no satisfactory solution to the ongoing demands of frequent travel. It is, in fact, draining. There are several things we can do, however, to make each journey as pleasant as it can possibly be.

To begin with, I suggest you become much friendlier to the flight attendants on your flights. I've been told dozens of times that I'm the friendliest passenger a flight attendant has "ever seen." This is a bit disturbing to me because, as a rule, I really don't enjoy flying and am probably at my *least* friendliest while on an airplane. What this tells me is that most of us are dreadfully impatient when we travel. Try to remember that flight attendants not only have to fly to earn their living, but they must try to keep you and me safe and comfortable, as well.

I've found that when I go out of my way to be kind, say thank you, and be appreciative and friendly, the time goes by much quicker and my flights are much more pleasant. When I'm friendly, the flight attendants are usually friendly, as well. They go out of their way to make my flight as pleasant as possible, and, I might be imagining it, but I think the other passengers seem to lighten up, too.

Do the same thing while waiting in ticket lines. You'll be amazed at how much nicer you are treated when you are nice first! I've been "mysteriously" bumped up to business or first class while holding an economy ticket—and given preferential seating (or a seat on a completely booked flight) on several occasions, simply because I was apparently the only passenger waiting in line who wasn't complaining or giving the ticket agents a bad time. While traveling on business, compassion and patience pay huge dividends.

Then there are the more obvious things. Try not to overeat on planes. Once in a while, I even skip my meal, and I'm always glad I did. If you must drink alcohol, try to keep it to a minimum. When you eat and drink too much on planes (and almost everyone I travel with does), it makes you feel groggy and listless. It makes your recovery much more difficult, and makes it harder to keep your weight under control.

Bring not just one, but several good books. While on planes, your mood can do strange things. It's a good time to read a book you might not normally think of reading. Use the flight time to try something different: a novel, for example, or a mystery. Or I've met people who have learned a foreign language while flying. They purchase an audio-cassette program, close their eyes, relax, and learn. I've been told that 100,000 miles later, they can speak French or Spanish!

Of course, you can always use the time to work. I'd guess that at least one-fourth of my writing for this book (ironically, not this section), was done on an airplane. Not in all cases, but almost always, there's a way to get some time-consuming, or as in my case, creative work done on planes. As I mentioned, I don't really like to fly. However, I've actually gotten to the point where I look forward to the work I *know* I'll get done on airplanes.

When you arrive at your destination, try to take advantage of whatever situation you are in. Have you ever wanted to learn to meditate or take up yoga? If so, what better place than in the solitude of a lonely and quiet hotel room? Have work to catch up on? Great, it's quiet and nondistracting. Try to get some exercise, even if it's in the room. Or, take a walk before your meetings or when you are done in the evening. I've found that hotel rooms are great places to catch up with old friends. I rarely, if ever, have time to make calls from home or the office. But occasionally in hotel rooms, I can sit in a comfortable chair and call an old friend.

I guess my bottom line is this: Make the best of it. Be creative. Invest in yourself. Take advantage of your situation. Rather than complain about your travel, try to make something of it. Someday, when you look back on your career, you will probably say one of two things. Either you'll say, "Gosh, I had to travel a lot and it was a nightmare." Or, you'll say, "Gosh, I had to travel a lot for work, but it was okay. I did everything I could to make the best of it." Either way, the travel will be over. The difference won't be in the number of days you traveled, or to what cities. Nor will it be in the number of frequent-flyer miles you accumulate. The difference will be in your attitude, nothing more. So, the next time you travel for business, make the best of it—and have a nice flight.

12.

LIGHT A CANDLE INSTEAD OF
CURSING THE DARKNESS

This is a strategy for better living that I have heard mentioned for many years. And while I sometimes forget to implement this wisdom, I try whenever possible to keep it in mind. It's extremely simple and reliable, yet often completely overlooked. As the title suggests, this strategy involves taking positive, solution-oriented steps (however small) toward improving a situation instead of complaining about what's wrong. It means being more a part of the solution rather than a reminder or reinforcement of the problem. I've found that work is the ideal environment to practice this philosophy.

While we're working, it's easy to fall into the trap of spending our time and energy taking note and complaining about the wrongs of the world—the way things are, the economy, negative people, industry changes, greed, lack of compassion, bureaucracy, and so forth. After all, if we are looking for verification that the world is full of problems, we don't have to look far to prove our assumptions.

If you take a careful look, you'll notice that in most cases, commiserating with others about the problems at work, or thinking excessively about them only serves to increase your own level of stress, thus making it even more difficult to do anything about the very things that are bothering you. As we focus on the problem and discuss it with others, it can reinforce our belief that life is difficult and stressful, which, of course, it can be. When we focus too much on what's wrong, it reminds us of other things we disapprove of or wish were different, which can lead us toward feelings of discouragement and being overwhelmed.

It's interesting, however, to notice that in many instances you cannot only make a dent in a problem, but actually reduce your own stress level in the process by simply choosing to "light a candle." Simply put, this means making a suggestion or taking a positive step toward improving a source of stress. It means putting increased emphasis on a potential solution and less emphasis on "cursing" the problem.

For example, suppose gossip or talking behind others' backs is a problem where you work. Rather than remaining resentful or frustrated that this bad habit exists, see if you can make a tiny dent in the problem. Gather together a few of your friends and gently bring the issue to the table. But rather than accusing anyone, focus on your own contribution. Confess that you have been as guilty as anyone else in indulging in occasional gossip, and state that you're going to make a genuine effort not to do so. Invite others to join you. Make your invitation lighthearted and unthreatening. Focus on the positive benefits of decreased gossip— nicer feelings toward one another, not having to worry so much about what others are saying about you, less stress, and so forth. In many cases, the people you work with will jump at the opportunity to join you—simply because you have taken the first step. Even if they don't, you will have taken a positive step toward the reduction of a nasty corporate habit. Either way, you win!

I met Sarah in the Department of Motor Vehicles. She was the most helpful employee I've ever seen in the role she was performing. In her line, which was moving quickly, people were smiling and leaving satisfied. She was friendly, courteous, and efficient. I couldn't resist asking her what her secret was. Here is what she said: "I spent several years putting customers off with the excuse, 'That's not my department.' The truth was, at least half the time, I knew the answer to the questions being asked, and in most cases could have been much more helpful. Virtually everyone in line was either mad at me or disgusted by my bureaucratic attitude. At some point I became fed up with my own sourpuss behavior and decided to change. Now, whenever possible, I help people out instead of putting them off and forcing them to wait in a different line. Everything has changed; most people appreciate me now. I feel better about myself, and my job is a lot more fun."

See how easy it is to light a candle?

13.

JOIN MY NEW CLUB, "TGIT"

Until now, the business world was primarily made of two clubs. The most popular club, by far, was the "TGIF" club, or "Thank God It's Friday." To be a member of this club, your primary focus is on the weekend. Members think about, anticipate, and look forward to Fridays so that they can get away from their work. Most members are highly stressed because only two days of the week are considered "good days." Even Sunday is considered a stressful day because the next day they have to go back to work.

The other business club is substantially smaller, yet in some ways the members are more dedicated to the club. This one is called "TGIM," or "Thank God It's Monday." These members are usually workaholics who can't stand weekends because they are away from work! Members of this club are also highly stressed because while there are generally five days of the week to be preoccupied with work, there is always that darn weekend that gets in the way! The most difficult day of the week is usually Friday, because it often means the member won't be able to get back to work for a few days. They may try to work on weekends, but the demands of family get in the way. Needless to say, members of both clubs think that members of the "other club" are completely nuts!

I invite you to join an alternate club. My hope is that together, we can eventually achieve a 100 percent membership. In fact, I'd love to put the other two clubs out of business altogether! This new club is called

"TGIT," or "Thank God It's Today." Members of this club are happy seven days a week because they understand that every day is unique, and each brings with it different gifts. Members of this club are grateful to be alive; they rejoice in their many blessings and expect each day to be full of wonder, surprise, and opportunity.

There are no qualifications necessary to join the "TGIT" club, other than the desire to have a higher quality of life and the desire to appreciate rather than dread each day. Members of this club understand that it's useless to wish any day were different. They know that Mondays don't care if you like them or not—they simply go on being Mondays. Likewise, Fridays will come around every seventh day, whether you wish it were Friday or not. It's up to each of us to make every day as special as it can be. No amount of wishing will make the slightest bit of difference.

As simple as it seems, the desire to maintain a membership in this club can make a substantial difference in the attitude you carry with you at work, and in fact in all of life. Just think: If you wake up every day of the week with an attitude of, "I'm glad today is today. I'm going to make this day as positive and wonderful as I possibly can," you may be surprised at how much less stressed you'll be. This simple shift of attitude goes a long, long way toward a more positive experience of life and work.

14.

DON'T SWEAT
THE DEMANDING BOSS

I'd estimate that a large percentage of adults that I know are either working for, or have worked for, a demanding boss. Like deadlines, taxes, and budgets, demanding bosses seem to be a fact of life for many working people. Even if you don't technically work "for" someone else, you may have demanding people that you work with or who pay your bills, or demanding customers you must attempt to please.

Like everything else, there are two ways to deal with demanding bosses. We can, like most do, complain about them, talk behind their backs, wish they would go away, secretly plot against them in our minds, wish them ill will, and feel forever stressed about the situation. Or we can take a different path and try (hard as it is) to stay focused on the positive aspects of the demanding party.

This was a particularly difficult concept for me to embrace, as I've always hated it when I feel pushed to perform. However, after dealing with many, many pushy people in my career, I've come to realize some important things.

The first "saving grace" I realized about demanding people is that, generally speaking, they are demanding to everyone. In other words, it's not personal. Before I recognized this to be the case, I would assume, as many do, that Mr. or Mrs. Demanding was "out to get me." I took their demanding demeanor personally and felt pressured. I would then compound the problem by thinking about his or her hidden motives, making a case within my own head as to why I had "a right to be angry." I would even go home at night and complain to poor Kris, who had already heard my story many times before.

All this began to change as I began to see a hint of innocence in the demanding party. In other words, I began to see that, in a very real sense, he or she really couldn't help it—they were stuck in the role of being demanding. This didn't change my preference for working with less-demanding people, but it did make it easier to accept when I had to.

I was working on a book a number of years ago when I was forced to work with a very demanding editor. I was having a difficult time with all the criticism and pushing, when a friend of mine asked me a very important question. She said, "Has it ever occurred to you that the most demanding people are often the ones who push you out of your comfort zone and help you rise to a new level of competence?" Until that moment, it hadn't occurred to me that this was true. As I look back at my career, I now realize that it was often the case that demanding people were the ones who brought out the best in me. Everything—from my writing style, to my ability to use a computer and adjust to technology, to my ability to speak in public—was greatly enhanced by my connection to demanding, even abrasive people.

Suzanne worked for someone who could only be described as "a real jerk." She described him as "a person who was demanding for no other reason than to be demanding." He seemed to feel a perverse sense of power when he was ordering people around.

Other than Suzanne, everyone in the office was either frightened or resentful of this demanding boss. For some reason, she had the wisdom to see through his huge ego and obnoxious behavior. Whenever possible, she tried to see the humor in her situation and instead of hating him, to see if there were things she might learn from his skills rather than focusing on his flaws. Her learning curve was sharp. It wasn't too long before her ability to stay cool in a hostile environment was noticed by her boss's employer, and she was promoted to a more interesting position in a different department.

The realization that there are two sides to demanding people—positive and negative—has made my entire life, especially my work life, a whole lot easier. Whereas before I would become defensive and dread the process, I now approach demanding people in an entirely new way. I'm open to what they may have to teach me, and I don't take their behavior personally. What has happened is quite remarkable. Because I'm so much less adversarial and defensive than I used to be, the "demanding" people I meet and work with seem to be a lot easier to be around. I now realize that my overreaction to demanding people had a lot to do with how difficult they were for me to deal with. As is so often the case, as I have grown and have been willing to open my mind to my own contribution to my problems, I have been rewarded with an easier life. I'm not advocating demanding behavior, as I still see it as a negative and abrasive personality trait. However, I have learned to take it in stride and see it as "small stuff." Perhaps the same can happen to you.

15.

REMEMBER TO ACKNOWLEDGE

I can't think of a single person who doesn't love and appreciate being acknowledged. On the flip side, most people either resent, or at least feel slighted by not being acknowledged. This being the case, this one seems like a "no-brainer."

You can acknowledge others in many ways. When someone calls you, acknowledge the call. When they send you something, remember to say thank you, or take the time to write a note. When someone does a good job, say so. When they apologize, acknowledge that too. It's especially important to acknowledge acts of kindness—doing so reinforces the act and encourages more of the same. We all benefit.

Almost everyone loves to be acknowledged. We love to have our phone calls returned, to be told we are doing a great job, to be thanked for working so hard, to have our creativity appreciated, to be reminded that we are special.

Approximately fifty people report to Dennis, who runs a large department in an insurance company. Dennis was in the habit of taking everyone for granted. His exact words to me were, "My philosophy used to be that people were lucky to have a job. I felt that if someone was doing a good job, their reward was one more paycheck." I encouraged him to think in a more loving, generous way and to expand his definition of acknowledgment. It took some time, but he was able to do so, genuinely and graciously.

As he looks back, he can hardly believe how he used to behave. He told me, "Everyone who worked for me was frightened and insecure, and no one felt appreciated. Today, I try to always remember to acknowledge a job well done. I can sense an enormous difference. People are lighter, happier, less defensive and more loyal than before. It will probably take more time, but I feel like people are starting to forgive me. I've learned that I need my employees as much as they need me."

We should acknowledge others, not simply to get something in return, but because it's the right thing to do—because it makes them feel good. I have to tell you, however, that in this case, "doing the right thing" really does come back to help you. It's difficult to quantify, but I'm certain that acknowledgment has played a critical role in my own success as a professional and as a human being. I've written hundreds of thank-you letters and made thousands of phone calls simply to acknowledge the acts of others. I know that I drop the ball every once in a while and that things do fall between the cracks, but my intention is to acknowledge everyone, when it's appropriate. Time and time again I've been praised and thanked for being "the only person who took the time to acknowledge."

People remember acknowledgment and they appreciate it. When you need a favor, or advice, the fact that you have previously taken the time to acknowledge someone often comes back to help you. It makes others want to help you and to see you succeed. Also, people who have been acknowledged genuinely and with love are very forgiving. They will see beyond your mistakes and failures and forgive you freely. Needless to say, all of this makes your life easier and far less stressful. So think about it. Does someone in your work life deserve some sort of acknowledgment? If so, what's holding you up?

16.

DON'T KEEP PEOPLE WAITING

One of the ways I attempt to keep my own stress under control is to avoid, whenever possible, the bad habit of keeping other people waiting. Time is precious to everyone. I've observed that almost everyone feels that one of their most valued commodities is their time. This being the case, one of the ultimate slaps and most surefire ways to annoy someone is to keep them waiting. While most people are somewhat forgiving, keeping them waiting is a sign of disrespect and a lack of acknowledgment. The subtle message is, "My time is more important than yours." Consider the magnitude of this suggestion. Do you feel that anyone else's time is more precious than yours? I doubt it. Doesn't it make sense then that everyone else feels the same way?

Deep down, we all know that noone likes to be kept waiting. Therefore, it's highly stressful to keep other people waiting because you know you are disappointing someone. In the back of your mind, you know darn well the person is looking at his watch, wondering where you are and why you are late. You may be keeping him from personal or professional commitments and that could make him angry or resentful.

There are obviously exceptions to the rule—times when factors beyond your control prevent you from being on time. Things happen to all of us, and noone has a perfect record. Truthfully, however, a vast majority of the time, being late is preventable. But instead of planning ahead, allowing a little extra time, or making allowances for unexpected problems, we wait just a little too long, or don't allow quite enough time—so we end up late. We then compound the problem by making excuses like "traffic was horrible," when, in reality, traffic is virtually always horrible. The problem wasn't traffic—but the fact that we didn't factor enough time in our schedule for the traffic. It's likely the case that, even if traffic was horrible, or you got off to a late start, or whatever the excuse, the other person isn't going to be interested or impressed. It may not be fair, but sometimes your work and other positive traits will be over-shadowed by the fact that you were late.

I wouldn't underestimate the negative impact of making someone wait. It drives some people crazy. And, even if they don't express their frustration to you directly, it can show up in other ways—not taking you as seriously, avoiding you when possible, being disrespectful, choosing to spend their time with others instead of you, showing up late to your future appointments, as well as an assortment of other forms of retaliation.

Even if you were somehow able to discount the effects of your show-ing up late, it still creates an enormous amount of stress in your life in other ways. When you're late, you're scrambling. You're in a hurry, behind schedule. It's difficult to be present-moment-oriented because you're concerned about whatever it is you're running late for. Your mind is filled up with stressful thoughts like, "What might happen?" or "I've done it again." Or you might be hard on yourself, wondering, "Why do I always have to run late?"

When you're on time, however, you avoid all this stress and then some. They may not express it, but the people you work with will appre-ciate the fact that you're not late. They won't have any reason to be mad at you or to think you don't respect their time. They won't be talking behind your back, and you won't get the reputation as the person who is always late. You'll stop rushing and, because you won't be so hurried, you'll relax a little bit and have slightly more time to reflect.

Some of my very best ideas have come to mind between appointments, when I've had a few minutes to be quiet, when I wasn't in a hurry. I've thought up solutions to problems, as well as ideas for a book or a speech that was coming up. It's clear to me that had I been rushing around, running late, it's likely the ideas would have been buried in the frazzle. I've met a number of people who confess that they used to keep people waiting—and who have seen their lives change for the better by implementing this very simple and courteous strategy. Perhaps it can help you as well.

17.

CREATE A BRIDGE BETWEEN
YOUR SPIRITUALITY
AND YOUR WORK

When I've suggested that spirituality become a more integral part of a person's life, I've often heard the reply, "I'd love for that to happen but I'm just too busy. I have to go to work." If that sounds familiar, this strategy may be helpful.

To create a bridge between your spirituality and your work means that you take the essence of who you are and what you believe into your daily work life. You dismantle the dichotomy that so often exists between your spiritual life and that which you do for a living. It means that if kindness, patience, honesty, and generosity are spiritual qualities that you believe in, you make every effort to practice those qualities at work. You treat people with kindness and respect. If someone is late or makes a mistake, you try to be patient. Even if it's your job or appropriate to reprimand someone, you do so from a place of love and respect. You are as generous as you can be—with your time, money, ideas, and love.

In a way, work is a perfect environment to practice your spirituality. In a given day, you have so many opportunities to practice patience, acts of kindness, and forgiveness. You have time to think loving thoughts, smile, embrace others, and practice gratitude. You can practice being nondefensive and a better listener. You can try to be compassionate, particularly with difficult or abrasive people. You can practice your spirituality in virtually everything that you do. It can be found in the way you greet people and deal with conflict. You can exhibit it in the way you sell a product or service—or the way you balance ethics with profit. It's literally everywhere.

Grace is a literary (book and related projects) agent. She is someone who, in my opinion, has created this bridge very well. In part, she describes her spiritual philosophy as one of "non-violence, integrity, and a love of all creatures." I have never seen an instance where she didn't "walk her talk." She turns down books and other potential projects when they conflict with her values, even when she is turning away guaranteed money. I've seen her walk away from an offer when questionable ethics were involved. She has told me, on more than one occasion, "I'd never sell myself short just to make money. I'm always able to look myself proudly in the mirror and know that I'm a person who can be trusted." I know she feels good about herself, as well she should. I'm proud to know her, as she is the type of person I admire and love to be around.

There's something really comforting about creating this spiritual bridge. It reminds you of a higher purpose. It puts your problems and concerns into a broader context. It helps you grow from your difficult experiences rather than become hopeless or overwhelmed by them. Even if you have to do something terribly difficult such as firing someone, for example, you do so while remembering your humanity. Or even if you are fired or dealt some other tremendous "blow" or hardship, there is a part of you that knows there is a reason. Having this faith helps you get through difficult times. It gives you confidence in a bigger picture. It doesn't mean that difficult times become easy—just a little more manageable.

One of the nicest things that happens to people as they create a bridge between their spirituality and their work is that "small stuff" really *does* begin to seem like small stuff. Invariably, the same things that used to drive you crazy won't seem at all significant. You'll be able to take things in stride, move forward, and stay focused. So, in a roundabout way, becoming more spiritual at work is going to help you become even more successful than you already are. I can't think of anything more important than creating a bridge between your spirituality and your work. Can you?

18.

BRIGHTEN UP YOUR
WORKING ENVIRONMENT

I wish I could include a photograph of my office in this book. It's bright, inviting, friendly looking, and peaceful. In fact, it's so happiness-oriented that it's almost impossible to get depressed while you're in it. Most people who visit fall in love with it and claim they almost always feel better when they leave. Yet I can assure you that my office is not fancy, and is certainly not expensively decorated.

There are tropical fish swimming in a tank, photographs of my wife and children, and several beautiful pictures that they drew for me. The pictures are in frames and are changed and updated every few months. The ones that are replaced are never thrown away, but put in a scrapbook that is proudly displayed. Every week I bring new freshly cut flowers to the office and put them in water. They are beautiful and smell terrific. My bookshelf is filled with many of my favorite books, and I look out on a birdfeeder that is heavily used. My kids have even been nice enough to share a few of their Beanie Babies with me, and they sit proudly on a shelf keeping me company. My favorite is a purple hippo named Happy.

I know that most people don't have the luxury or permission to turn their office into a "happiness headquarters." I also know that my office, while appropriate for me, would not be appropriate for or even preferred by many others. That's all well and good. However, when I enter the working environment of many people, my immediate thought is, "No wonder this person feels so stressed-out." Many offices, cubicles, work stations, home offices, and other working environments are downright depressing. They're bland, boring, dark, and lack any creativity whatsoever. Many are completely void of any signs of life, happiness, gratitude, relationships, or nature.

Brightening up your working environment will not rid you of all your stress, nor is it the most important thing you can do to stop sweating the small stuff at work. However, you do spend an enormous amount of time where you work. Why not take a tiny bit of time, energy, and money and brighten it up, even a little? When I moved into my office, the carpet was thin, ugly, and dark. For a few hundred dollars, I bought a beautiful new carpet that really looks nice and feels good to walk on. If I'm in the same office for even five years, that amounts to a few cents per day. I believe I'm the only person in my entire office building to have invested in myself in this way. Sometimes it's interesting how little we value ourselves.

If you aren't able to do it yourself, perhaps you can ask someone to help you—a spouse, a friend, a coworker, even a child! You might be surprised at how easy it is. Try a few pictures, a brighter rug, inspirational books, freshly cut flowers, goldfish, signs of nature, or some combination. You'd be amazed at what a drawing from a child can do to lift your spirits. If you don't have kids, maybe someone you work with would be kind enough to share one with you. Even if you work in your car or drive a truck, there are little things you can do to make your environment a nicer place to be.

I once heard the brilliant comedian Steve Martin joking about how difficult it is to feel depressed while you're playing the banjo. He was singing about death and sorrow. As he strummed the strings, it was obviously that he was right. There's something about that particular sound that is inconsistent with sadness and grief—it sounds too happy. To some extent, the same is true of your working environment. It's really nice to walk in and feel good about where you are going to spend your day. Make it bright, cheery and friendly, and it's pretty hard to walk in and not feel the same way.

19.

TAKE YOUR BREAKS

One of the worst habits I developed early on in my career was my failure to take adequate breaks. I'm a little embarrassed to admit it, but I felt they were a waste of time. I assumed that by skipping my breaks unless it was absolutely necessary, I'd be able to save a great deal of time and get more done—I'd have an edge. I'd work through lunch and rarely take breaks throughout the day.

In recent years, I've learned that a failure to take regular breaks is an enormous mistake that not only wears you down over time, but actually makes you less productive. While you may not even feel it at the time, slowly but surely your frustration will sneak up on you. You'll become less patient and attentive, and your concentration and listening skills will suffer. I believe that the cumulative effects, over time, are also significant. You'll burn out much more quickly, and your creativity and insights will slowly fade away.

It can be subtle, but when I pay careful attention to what's going on inside myself, I can tell that the same things that don't get to me very much when I'm well-rested and take my breaks somehow start to annoy me a little when I don't. I'll be a little less patient and lose a little of my enthusiasm. I start to sweat the small stuff—a little more than before. It seems to me that, while everyone certainly has a different rhythm and different capacities to work without breaks, there is something nourishing and healing to the spirit that occurs when you take a few minutes for yourself, whether or not you feel you need it.

Your breaks don't have to be disruptive or last very long. Usually, all you need is a few minutes to clear your head, take some deep breaths, stretch your arms, or get some air. When you take this time—every hour, or so—you'll return to your work more enthusiastic, focused, and ready to go. It's almost as though you push a "reset button" and you provide yourself with a fresh start. Often after taking a short break, my wisdom and creativity are enhanced, and I'm able to produce some of my best results.

Like most people, occasionally I forget to take my breaks. I'll sit for hours in essentially the same position writing a chapter or working on a project. Eventually when I get up, I feel stiff and tired. Then it hits me: "I forgot to take a break." There have been exceptions, but usually when I look back on my work, I'll be able to tell it wasn't my best effort.

This strategy reinforces the idea that more isn't always better. I feel that by working a few less minutes each hour, I'll work smarter, more efficiently, and actually get more work accomplished. And because of all the energy I'm saving on a day-to-day basis, I may even add a few years to the life of my career.

I suppose it's time to practice what I preach. I'll close this section by telling you that I'm going to take a short break. Perhaps this would be a good time for you to take one as well.

20.

DON'T TAKE THE 20/80
RULE PERSONALLY

According to the 20/80 "rule," it's allegedly the case that in the work-place, 20 percent of the people do approximately 80 percent of the work. When I'm in a cynical mood, it sometimes seems that this ratio is grossly understated!

It's often the case that people who are highly productive or who have an intense work ethic don't understand why everyone else isn't just like them. It can be frustrating for these people to observe, work with, or in some cases, even be in the presence of people whom they perceive to be less productive than they should be—people who appear to get less done than they could. For some reason, they take it personally and allow it to bother them.

I've observed that many "overachievers" don't even see themselves as achievers—but rather as ordinary people who simply do what it takes to succeed or get the job done. They honestly don't understand why every-one isn't just like them. I once knew a super-achieving man who insist-ed, "I'm not an overachiever. It's just that most people are underachiev-ers." I knew him well enough to know that he wasn't intentionally being arrogant. Rather, he was sharing with me the way he really saw the world. He honestly felt that most people don't work hard enough and almost no one lives up to their full potential. If you really believed this to be true, you can imagine how frustrated and irritated you would be most of the time. You'd be programmed to see everything that wasn't getting done, or that could or should be done differently. You would see the world in terms of its deficiencies.

You may not have such an extreme vision (I certainly don't), but you too may see the world from highly productive, efficient eyes. If so, it may be hard to accept (or understand) that other people have different priorities, work ethics, comfort levels, gifts, abilities, and mind-sets. People see things from entirely different perspectives and work at vastly different speeds. Remember, different people also define productivity in very different ways.

An easy way to come to peace with this productivity issue is to pay less attention to what other people *aren't* doing, and put more emphasis on what you get out of your own level of productivity—financially, energetically, emotionally, even spiritually. In other words, it's helpful to admit that you prefer to be a highly productive individual—it's your choice. And along with this choice comes certain benefits. You may feel better about yourself than if you were less productive, or feel that you are fulfilling your mission or living up to your potential. Perhaps you make more money, or enjoy your work more than you would if you were less productive. You may have a more financially secure future, or an increased likelihood of opening certain doors for yourself. Or you may alleviate anxiety by getting a certain amount of work done each day. In other words, you have a number of payoffs that are driving you. Therefore, you are not a victim of those people who make different choices, or who, for whatever reason, aren't as productive as you, at least according to your standards.

To put this issue into perspective, it's helpful to think about your own work ethic, preferred pace of work, and overall ability to get things done. Ask yourself these questions: "Do I base my productivity choices on what others think I should be doing?" "Am I attempting to frustrate and irritate others by the pace of my work?" Of course not. Your choices are the result of your own rhythm, preferred pace of work, and desired results. Although you may be required to perform at a certain level, your overall productivity level stems from your own decisions and perceived payoffs.

The same is true for everyone else. It's not personal—it's not about you or me. Each person decides from within him or herself how much work is appropriate, all things considered. Everyone must weigh the pros and cons, consider the tradeoffs, and decide how hard they are going to work—and how productive they are going to be.

You may depend on other people—colleagues, coworkers, subcontractors, employees—to adhere to certain standards and levels of productivity. I certainly do. I'm not suggesting that you ease up or that you lower your standards. Instead, I'm suggesting that there's a way to look at varying levels of productivity in a healthy and productive way that can keep you from getting so upset and from taking it personally. I've found that when I'm able to maintain my perspective, and keep my own stress level under control, it's easy for me to bring out the absolute best in people without making them feel defensive or resentful.

I encourage you to examine your own subtle demands and expectations that others work the way you do. Once you accept the fact that it's not personal, you'll probably be able to lighten up enough to appreciate the differences in people and the way they choose to work. If so, you're going to feel more peaceful and relaxed.

21.

MAKE A LIST OF YOUR
PERSONAL PRIORITIES

I'll warn you in advance that this strategy can be humbling, but ultimately very helpful. It involves taking a careful look at those personal things that you feel are most important to you. Once you decide what they are, write them down on a sheet of paper and put the list away for a week or two.

For example, you might create a list that looks something like this: 1. pleasure reading, 2. exercise, 3. volunteering my time, 4. spending time with my family or close friends, 5. meditation, 6. spending time in nature, 7. getting organized, 8. writing in my journal, 9. trying something new, 10. eating healthily, 11. traveling.

Here's the hard part: after some time has gone by, take out your list and read it to yourself. Now, think back honestly over the past week or so, back to the time you wrote the list. How have you spent your time, other than the time you were working? If your actions over the past few weeks were consistent with your list, congratulations! You are in a tiny minority, and my only suggestion is to encourage you to keep it up. My guess is that you are fairly satisfied in your life, and that satisfaction spills over into your work life.

If, however, you look at your list and realize (as I did the first time I did this exercise) that a staggering percentage of your time was spent doing other things, then you've got work to do. If you're like most people, you probably got little or no exercise, didn't get around to volunteering, and spent all your time inside. To varying degrees, we ignore that which we insist is more important in favor of things that seem pressing or are simply more convenient. Unfortunately, life isn't going to suddenly accommodate us with fewer demands or reward us with the time we wish we had to do these important things. If we don't line up our behavior with our priorities, it will never happen.

A friend of mine taught me a powerful lesson that I always try to remember. He said, "In reality, you vote with your actions, not your words." This means that while I can tell you that my friends and family are important to me, I can write well-intended lists, and I can even become defensive in my well-thought-out excuses, ultimately, the measure of what's most important to me is how I spend my time and energy.

To put it bluntly, if I spend my free time washing my car, drinking in bars, and watching TV, then presumably my car, alcohol, and my TV are what's most important to me.

This isn't to say there is anything wrong with these activities—it's just important to admit to yourself that this is how you've been spending your time. It's also not to say that there aren't times when watching TV, even washing the car, is the most important thing to you at that moment. Again, that's fine. What I'm referring to here are your patterns of behavior, the way you spend most of your time.

You can see why this exercise is potentially so important to the quality of your life. When you're busy and working hard, tired and overwhelmed, it's easy to postpone or overlook your true priorities. You can get so lost in your routine and busyness that you end up doing few or none of the things that, deep down, you know would nourish you. You tell yourself things like, "This is a particularly busy time," or "I'll get to it later," but you never get around to it. This lack of satisfaction translates into frustration at work and elsewhere.

Once you open your eyes to the pattern, however, it's fairly easy to change. You can begin to make minor adjustments. You can read a few minutes before you go to sleep, get up a little earlier to exercise, meditate, or read. And so on. Remember, you're the one who wrote the list of priorities. You certainly have the power to implement them. I encourage you to write your list today—it really can create a whole new beginning.

22.

USE EFFECTIVE LISTENING AS
A STRESS-REDUCING TOOL

I've written about various aspects of listening in most of my previous books. The reason I return to listening so often is that, in my opinion, it's one of the most important ingredients for success in virtually all aspects of life—personal and professional. Unfortunately, for many of us, it's also one of our greatest weaknesses. Yet the slightest improvement in our listening skills can pay enormous dividends in the way of better relationships, enhanced performance, and yes, even stress reduction!

Take a moment to reflect on your own listening skills at work. Do you truly listen to your colleagues? Do you let them finish their thoughts before you take your turn? Do you sometimes finish sentences for other people? In meetings, are you patient and responsive—or are you impatient and reactive? Do you allow words from others to sink in, or do you assume you know what the person is trying to say, so you jump in? Simply asking yourself these and related questions can be enormously helpful. Most people I've asked (I'm in this category too), admit that, at least some of the time, their listening skills could use a little improvement.

There are a variety of reasons why effective listening is an excellent stress-reducing technique. First of all, people who listen well are highly respected and sought after. Truly great listeners are so rare that when you are around one, it feels good, it makes you feel special. Since effective listeners are loved by the people they work with (and the people they live with), they avoid many of the most common stressful aspects of work—backstabbing, resentment, sabotage, and ill feelings. Good listeners are easy to be around, so, quite naturally, you want to reach out and help them. Therefore, when you become a better listener, there will probably be plenty of people in your corner to offer assistance. People tend to be loyal to good listeners because they feel acknowledged and respected.

Effective listening helps you to understand what people are saying the first time they say it, thus allowing you to avoid a great number of mistakes and misinterpretations which, as you know, can be very stressful. If you ask people what frustrates them and makes them angry, many will tell you that "not being listened to" is right near the top of their lists. So, being more attentive to what others are saying also helps you avoid many, if not most, interpersonal conflicts. Finally, effective listening is an enormous time-saver because it helps you eliminate sloppy mistakes. Instructions as well as concerns from others become crystal clear, thus helping fend off unnecessary, time-consuming errors.

This is one of those powerful strategies that can generate immediate and significant results. You may have to work at it a little but if you do, it will be well worth it. The people you work with may not be able to put their finger on exactly what it is that you're doing differently, but they will notice a difference in how they feel when they are around you, or when they are speaking to you. And, in addition to being more liked and admired, you'll find yourself becoming calmer and more peaceful as well.

23.

MAKE FRIENDS WITH
YOUR RECEPTIONIST

Not too long ago I was in San Francisco in a reception lounge, wait-ing for my lunch partner. I was lucky enough to be a witness to the following chain of events which were so to the point of this book, I imme-diately knew I would like to share them with you.

A man walked in and barked out, in an unfriendly and demanding tone, "Any messages?" The female receptionist looked up and smiled. In a pleasant tone she answered, "No, sir." He responded in a nasty, almost threatening manner, "Just be sure to call me when my twelve-thirty appointment arrives. Got it?" He stormed down the hall.

No more than a minute later, a woman entered the room who appar-ently also wanted to know if she had any messages. She smiled, said "hello," and asked the receptionist if she was having a nice day. The receptionist smiled back and thanked the woman for asking. She then proceeded to hand the woman a stack of messages and shared with her some additional information which I could not hear. They laughed together a few times before the woman thanked the receptionist and walked down the hall.

It's always shocked me when I've seen someone who isn't friendly to the receptionist or who takes him or her for granted. It seems like such an obviously short-sided business decision. Over the years I've asked many receptionists whether or not they treat everyone in the office equally. Most of the time I receive a response such as, "You're kidding, right?" Indeed, it seems that receptionists have a great deal of power—and being friendly to them can make your life a lot easier. Not only does being nice to your receptionist all but ensure a friendly hello and someone to trade smiles with a few times a day, but in addition, your receptionist can do a great many intangible things for you—protect your privacy and screen calls, remind you of important events, alert you to potential problems, help you prioritize and pace yourself, and on and on.

I've seen both ends of the spectrum. I've seen receptionists protect people they work with from a variety of unnecessary hassles, even save them from major mistakes. I once saw a receptionist run down the hall and all the way down the street to remind someone of a meeting she was sure the person was going to forget. I later asked the person who was chased to tell me what had happened. He verified that the receptionist had been his "hero." He went so far as to claim that she may have even saved his job. When I asked this receptionist about their rapport, she informed me that they weren't really friends, but that he was an extremely nice person. I asked her if that had anything to do with her willingness to run down the street in the hot sun to remind him of a meeting. She just smiled and said, "You get right to the point, don't you?"

Sadly, the opposite can occur when a receptionist feels taken for granted or resentful of someone. I've heard stories of receptionists who have mysteriously "lost" messages, or who have failed to remind someone of a meeting, because it was inconvenient to do so.

Obviously, there are plenty of great receptionists who are able to set aside their personal feelings and do what is best, most if not all of the time. But think about this issue from the perspective of the receptionist. He or she might answer the phone, respond to the messages for a relatively large number of people, and have a number of other important responsibilities. Some of the people they work with are really nice, most are moderately so, and a few are jerks. Isn't it obvious that being friendly to your receptionist is in your best interest? Aside from the fact that it's their job, what possible motivation does a receptionist have to go the extra mile, or do something they aren't officially being paid to do, if you aren't nice to them—or at very least respectful?

In no way am I suggesting that you make friends with your receptionist just to get something in return. Primarily, you want to do so simply because it's a nice thing to do and because it will brighten the workday for both of you. After all, your receptionist is someone you see on a daily basis. But aside from that, it's just good business and it takes so little time or effort. My suggestion is to think of your receptionist as a key partner in your life. Treat them as if you truly value them—as you should. Be kind, genuine, patient, and courteous. Thank them when they do something for you—even if it's part of their job. Can you imagine the stress and other possible consequences of missing just one of those important phone calls—or a single important message? It's your receptionist who prevents that from happening. Wouldn't it seem wise to include your receptionist on your holiday shopping list? Incidentally, the same principle applies to many other roles as well, in different ways—the janitor, housecleaner, managers, cook, and so on.

I think you'll find that making friends with your receptionist is a wise thing to do. It's a great way to brighten your day-to-day work life, as well as an effective way to make your life a little less stressful. If you haven't already done so, I encourage you to give it a try.

24.

REMEMBER THE MOTTO,
"YOU CATCH MORE FLIES
WITH HONEY"

When I see someone badgering another person, acting aggressively or intimidating someone, pushing their weight around, or being mean-spirited or manipulative, I feel like reminding them that, in the long run, you really do catch more flies with honey. Simply put, it pays to be nice! Sure, there are times when being pushy or aggressive will assist you in getting your way—you can scare or intimidate certain people some of the time. But I believe that this type of aggressive attitude and behavior almost always comes back to haunt you.

When you are kind, loving, and patient—when you are fair, a good listener, and when you genuinely care about others—your attitude comes across in all you do. As a result, people love to be around you and will be comfortable and trusting in your presence. They side with you, share their secrets of success, and want to assist you in any way they can. Very simply, they delight in your success. When you are gentle, people are drawn to you like "flies to honey." They forgive you easily when you make a mistake and are willing to give you the benefit of the doubt. When they talk about you behind your back, their comments will be positive and upbeat. You will have a notable reputation.

It's unfortunate, but the opposite is also true. When you're difficult or demanding, your positive qualities are often overlooked, disregarded, or forgotten. In addition, you create a great deal of stress for yourself with an adversarial, aggressive attitude. You'll be looking over your shoulder wondering who, if anyone, is on your side. When you're pushy, you actually push people away. But when you're gentle and kind, people are drawn to your energy and sincerity.

I acknowledge that the "bottom line" is important and must be taken into consideration. That being said, I often make business decisions based not so much on cost, quality, or how much I'm being paid, as much as I do on how nice or pleasant someone is to work with. I've always felt that if I follow my heart and surround myself with great people, my experiences will be generally positive. I'll develop a healthy reputation with people who will like me, and my business decisions and relationships will develop and flourish into successful ventures. So far, my assumptions have been extremely accurate.

I've met a number of people who have said something like, "I'll never hire that person again." When I've asked, "Weren't you happy with his work?" they will usually say, "Absolutely. That's not it at all. It's just that he is so difficult to work with."

Chelsea is a hard-working, driven, and talented woman who works in retail. However, she is also very generous and kind. One of the many difficult aspects of retail work can be the long hours, particularly during weekends and holidays. Often, employees compete for time off and are very protective of the most sacred holidays.

When Chelsea began her career she decided that, despite what many people believe about being "walked on," gentleness and kindness were usually the most effective ways to behave. In her efforts to be kind, she was often willing to take someone else's shift so that they could spend time with family over an important holiday.

One day, Chelsea was given the extraordinary "once in a lifetime" opportunity to travel through Europe for two exciting months. In her position, however, it wasn't possible to take an extended trip without losing her job, unless she could somehow find a way to cover her extended time off. She had worked hard to achieve her position, and didn't want to "start over."

Much to her delight, her reputation allowed her to take the trip *and* keep her job. Her fellow employees jumped at the opportunity to come to her rescue. With tears in her eyes, she described it as "the most incredible, unselfish act by a group of people she had ever seen at work."

I think it's important to consider this strategy even if you feel you are a relatively gentle person. Most of us—certainly I include myself—have a long way to go. We might be doing okay, but, without even realizing it, still push others around from time to time, act a little arrogant, try to guilt them into doing certain things, or use other tools of manipulation to get our way. When we reflect on the practical, real-life importance of being gentle and patient, we can become even more so. I'd like to believe that, on an intuitive level, most people already know that you catch more flies with honey. Nevertheless, I think it's a good reminder for all of us.

25.

AVOID THE PHRASE,
"I HAVE TO GO TO WORK"

I'm going to suggest a strategy that has to do with six of the most common words in the English language: "I have to go to work."

Before I continue, let me assure you that I'm aware that in all probability, it's absolutely true that you do "have to" go to work. Nevertheless, these particular words carry with them some really negative baggage that, I believe, is self-destructive.

Other than your thoughts, your words are your primary entry point into your experience. They paint a picture of your expectation and pave the way toward your experience. When you "have" to do something, it implies that it's not a choice—that you'd rather be somewhere else, doing something different. This, in turn, implies that your heart isn't fully into what you are doing, which makes living up to your potential extremely difficult and enjoying your experience near impossible. So, when you say, "I have to go to work," you are in a subtle way setting yourself up for a bad day. This doesn't mean you'll always have a bad day—but it certainly increases the likelihood.

Beyond that, however, there is a more subtle negative message you send to yourself and to others. It seems that deep down, what you're really saying is, "I don't like my work. I'm not capable of choosing work that I enjoy." What a horrible message to say to yourself (or to someone else) about something you spend most of your time doing! Think about it. If you really loved your work, why would you be saying, "I have to go to work"? Do you say, "I have to start my weekend now"? Wouldn't it make more sense to be saying, "I get to go to work," or "I'm off to earn my livelihood," or "I'm off to another day," or something even simpler like, "I'm off to work," without the attached negativity? I'm not suggesting you jump for joy or yell out, "Yippee, I get to go to work," but can't you come up with something just a little more upbeat to begin your day? Wouldn't you be just a little prouder of yourself? And don't you think it would be more pleasant for others to hear these more positive words? When I leave for work in the morning, for example, I don't want to send the message to my children, however subtle, that "work is a bummer and here I go again." Yuck!

I think you're going to be surprised at what may happen if you choose to implement this strategy. When you take this strategy to heart, as you habitually mumble "I have to go to work" in your typical grouchy mode, you begin to catch yourself doing so. This makes you smile or laugh at yourself because you now see how ridiculous it is. Then, as you rephrase your statement to something slightly more positive, it seems to send a subtle reminder to your brain that your expectation is that you're going to have a good day. Wouldn't you agree that, more often than not, your expectations tend to come true? When you expect to have a bad experience, you usually do. And when you expect to have a good one, you very seldom disappoint yourself.

If nothing else, I hope you'll at least ask yourself the question, "What possible value could these words have to the overall experience of my work day?" Keep in mind that most people spend a minimum of eight hours a day, five days a week, working. It's something you're going to do regardless of how you choose to verbalize it to yourself and to others. Why not get yourself off to a good start by avoiding the tendency to bad-mouth what you are about to do?

26.

BE AWARE OF THE
POTENTIALLY STRESSFUL
EFFECTS OF YOUR PROMISES

It wasn't until a few years ago that I began to realize how often I made subtle promises to people during the course of a given day—and how often I regretted doing so. It was surprising to discover that my need to make promises was playing a key role in my feelings of stress. Once I saw how I was contributing to my own feelings of being overwhelmed, it was relatively easy to make some minor adjustments in my behavior and reduce the overall stress in my work life.

Think about some of the promises we make to others that may not even seem like promises, or that we make semi-unconsciously. Statements like, "I'll call you later today," "I'll stop by your office," "I'll send you a copy of my book next week," "I'd be happy to pick that up for you," or, "Call me if you ever need me to take your shift." In a more subtle way, even innocent comments like, "No problem," can get you into trouble because this can be perceived as an offer to do something that, deep down, you may not really want or be able to do. In fact, you have just allowed that person to ask you to do even more for her because you told her it's not a problem.

I used to engage in this habit virtually every day. Someone would ask me to do something simple like, "Can you send me a copy of that article you were talking about?" I'd automatically say, "Sure, no problem." I'd even write myself a note so I wouldn't forget. However, by the end of the day or week, I'd have an entire page of promises that now needed to be delivered. I'd often regret making so many promises. Sometimes I'd even feel resentful. I was so busy trying to deliver on my promises, I'd often be short of time or forced to hurry on things I really needed to do.

If you're at all like me, you probably try really hard to keep your promises. Obviously, the more promises you make, the more pressure you have to keep them. At some point, if you make enough promises, it's almost inevitable that you'll feel stressed out in your attempts to keep everyone happy.

Let me be very clear about something. I'm not suggesting you stop making promises, or that many promises aren't necessary or important. Many are. What I'm suggesting is that a certain percentage of your promises (maybe even a small percentage) probably don't need to be made in the first place. And if they're not made, you will have less pressure to keep them! I know, for example, that I've often told my publisher, "I promise to get this to you by this time next week," when the truth is, they weren't expecting a promise—only my best effort. But now that the promise has been made, I'm almost forced to do whatever is necessary to stick to my word. Had I not made the promise, but instead simply done the best I could, there would have been less pressure on me. This is pretty subtle stuff, and no one thing is likely to create all that much stress, but cumulatively it really adds up.

I have learned to evaluate each request that is made to me and each offer that I make to others. For example, if I'm asked for that copy of an article that I mentioned earlier, I may offer to send it—or I might suggest an alternate way for the person making the request to obtain it. Sometimes it's appropriate to make a promise, and other times it's not.

I've also learned to make slightly fewer unsolicited offers to do things for people. In other words, rather than saying, "Hey, I'll send you a copy of that book we were discussing," as is my tendency, I sometimes resist making the offer out loud. That way, I can (and often do) still go ahead and send the book if I still feel like it later and have the time to do so, but I'm not obligated.

There are two major advantages to paying attention to the effect of your promises. First, it will save you a great deal of time and energy. Some of the promises you make are unnecessary and unappreciated. Others, you simply don't have the time to keep. One of the most precious assets we have is our time. In fact, a lack of time is one of the most consistent complaints that people share with me about their work. Everyone seems to agree that there's rarely enough time to get everything done. When you make fewer promises, you'll have more time to do that which is most relevant to you.

The other advantage to making fewer promises is that the promises you do make will mean more to you and to the people you are promising. You'll take extra care to attend to those promises that mean the most to you and those you love. If you are burdened by too many promises, it's easy to lose sight of what's most important. You usually end up breaking promises to those you love most. However, with less on your plate, you can keep things in perspective and keep your priorities straight. I won't *promise* this strategy is going to help you—but I suspect that it probably will.

27.

EXAMINE YOUR RITUALS AND HABITS (AND BE WILLING TO CHANGE SOME OF THEM)

When you work for a living, it's very easy to get into certain habits—some good, some not so good; some out of necessity, some out of default; some just because everyone else seems to be doing so; and some simply because you've "always done it that way." Many of these habits become so much a part of us that we never seem to question, much less change them. Often we'll begin a habit and continue it for our entire career.

Taking a close look at some of these habits and rituals, and being willing to change a few of them, can pay huge dividends in the quality of your life. Our habits are often enormous sources of stress in and of themselves. Because they create so much stress (with or without our knowledge), they can make the rest of our life seem even more stressful than it already does.

Here are a few common habits and rituals, among hundreds of possibilities. Some of these may sound familiar, others may not: You may be in the habit of not allowing yourself enough time to get ready before work, and are always in a hurry. You may be in the habit of eating a large lunch, yet complain of not having any time to exercise or always feeling tired in the afternoon. Perhaps you commute in your car—but have other options like a train or bus, which would be cheaper and would allow you to read or relax. Maybe you drink too much caffeine and feel nervous and agitated a great deal of the time. Perhaps you head for a bar after work for a few drinks, or have wine or other alcohol as part of your ritual at home. Maybe you're a little grumpy or argumentative in the morning instead of being friendly to the people you work with, which makes them hesitant to be helpful or creates unnecessary resentment. Maybe you spend too much time reading the newspaper, yet rarely allow time for your favorite book. Perhaps you go to bed too late in the evening—or too early. Or that late night snack that is supposed to be a form of relaxation may be interfering with the quality of your sleep. Only you know which, if any, habits are making your life more difficult.

You can see that any one of these habits has the potential to create a great deal of stress in your life—making your day harder and encouraging you to sweat the small stuff at work. That being the case, the willingness to examine your habits can almost always be a helpful exercise.

Let's explore, very briefly, how changing a few of the above examples might help reduce the stress in your life. Despite the apparent simplicity, they are powerful changes to make. Instead of saying to yourself, "I could never do that," open your mind and imagine making a change!

Often the difference between a stressful day and one that is satisfying or manageable is simply a question of whether or not you're in a constant hurry, particularly first thing in the morning. Getting up an hour earlier, or simply beginning the process of getting ready a little earlier, can make a world of difference.

I've known many people who have substituted a one-hour walk for their usual midday meal. Their lives have been transformed by this single decision. They have lost weight and became much healthier. They feel better and have far more energy. They are saving money on lunch and investing that money in their future. They often meet friends for their walk, thus turning it into a social hour. They feel more relaxed and calmer than at any point in their entire lives.

Many people who drink regularly feel sluggish and grumpy the next day. Quitting, or even cutting back, can make you feel better than you've ever thought possible. You may sleep better and have tons of extra energy during the day. You'll probably lose weight and spend less money as well, as alcohol is certainly an expensive habit. Most people who cut back their alcohol consumption feel that they are more patient and that their relationships improve as well.

If you commute in your car, you may have other options. I know people who have made the decision to take the train (or other types of transportation) instead of their car, and have benefited greatly by doing so. Instead of gripping the wheel and feeling frustrated, they use the time to read or listen to tapes. They nap, meditate, think, or simply relax.

Obviously, these are only a small handful of potential changes you might consider. Everyone is different, and we all have different habits that get in the way of our happiness. While I have no idea which habits you may want to change, I'm relatively certain you can think of at least one. Give it a try. What have you got to lose—except perhaps a little stress?

28.

STAY FOCUSED IN THE NOW

Much has been written about the magical quality of "being in the moment." I believe, however, that this is one of those evergreen bits of wisdom that you can never quite get enough of. As you train your attention to be more focused in this moment, you will notice some remarkable benefits occurring in your work life. You'll be far less stressed-out and hurried, more efficient, and easier to be with. You'll also enjoy your work more than ever before, become a much better listener, and will sharpen your learning curve.

So often, our attention wanders off into the future. We think (and worry) about many things all at once—deadlines and potential problems, what we're going to do this weekend, reactions to our work. We anticipate objections and hassles and things that are likely to go wrong. We often convince ourselves how difficult something is going to be, well in advance of the actual event.

Or our attention is drawn to the past—we regret a mistake we made last week, or an argument we had this morning. We sometimes fret about "last quarter's poor earnings," or relive a painful or embarrassing event. And whether it's in the future or the past, we usually find a way to imagine the worst. A great deal of this mental activity is about things in the future that may or may not ever happen. And even if they do, the anticipation of it is usually worse that the actual event, and is rarely helpful. Or it's about past activities that are over and done with; things that may have actually happened, but that we no longer have any control over.

All of this mental activity is happening, of course, while we are supposedly working. But how effective are we, really, when our minds are practically everywhere except right here?

I've done it both ways—worked while my mind is spinning every which way and while my mind is very focused—and I can tell you with absolute certainty that a focused mind is more relaxed, creative, and efficient than one that is scattered. I'd say that one of my greatest strengths is my ability (that is still in progress) to stay focused on one thing at a time. Whether I'm on the phone with someone or with them in person, I'm usually able to be "right there" with them without being distracted by other things. This allows me to really hear and understand what is being said.

I try to do the same thing when I'm writing. Short of an actual emergency, I'm completely absorbed in what I'm working on. This allows all of my available attention and energy to be directed to one single activity— an ideal environment for creativity and effective work. I've found that a single hour of truly focused work is at least equal in productivity to a full day of distraction. The same is true when I'm speaking to a group. One of the things I've worked really hard to achieve is the ability to be with a group of people without ever wishing I were somewhere else. In other words, if I'm in Chicago, I'm not thinking about tomorrow's engagement in Cleveland. I believe this present-moment orientation has made me a far more effective speaker and has allowed me to work very hard and travel a great deal without feeling overly exhausted.

This quality of "being in the moment" has far more to do with what's going on in your mind than on what's going on in your office. There will always be external distractions—phone calls, interruptions, appointments, and so forth. The key element is how quickly you can bring your attention back to what you are doing, going from one thing to the next and back again.

Even more than increased effectiveness, however, the greatest benefit of being fully present is that your work will become much more enjoyable. There is something truly magical about getting completely absorbed in what you are doing. It increases your satisfaction immensely. I'm sure you're going to enjoy this one.

29.

BE CAREFUL WHAT
YOU ASK FOR

Many of us spend a great deal of time wishing things were different. We dream of a "better job," more responsibility, less of this, and more of that. Sometimes, the things we spend our energy longing for actually do (or would) improve the quality of our life. Other times, however, the very things we wish for are hardly worth the tradeoffs, or the effort. For this reason, I suggest you be really careful what you ask for.

The purpose of this strategy isn't to encourage you to stop dreaming of, or working toward, a better life, but to remind you that sometimes your life is pretty darn good exactly the way it is. My goal here is to remind you to carefully think through what it is you think you want, because you just might end up getting it, which is often more than you bargained for—more frustration, more grief, more travel, more responsibility, more conflict, more demands on your time, and so forth. When you think in these terms, it often helps you reconnect with your gratitude and realize that perhaps things aren't as bad as we sometimes make them out to be.

I've met plenty of people who spent years focused on how much better their lives were going to be when certain things occurred—i.e., when they were finally promoted to various positions—so much so that they took for granted the good parts of the position they already had. In other words, they were so focused on what was wrong with their careers that they failed to enjoy and appreciate the gifts they were enjoying all along.

For example, a man I knew dreamed of a job he felt would be "so much better" within the same company he was working with. He lobbied for that job for quite some time, constantly complaining about his current position. It wasn't until he finally secured that job that he realized the major tradeoffs that were involved. It was true that he had a bit more prestige and a slightly better salary, yet he was now forced to travel several days a week, often much more often than that. He missed his three kids terribly and started missing important events—soccer games, music performances, teacher conferences, and other special dates. In addition, his relationship with his wife became strained as their relatively peaceful routine was set aside for the alleged "better life." He was also forced to scale way back on his much-loved exercise routine due to his busier, less flexible schedule.

A woman I knew worked hard to convince her boss that she deserved to telecommute instead of coming into the office. She succeeded. The problem was, she never realized (until a month later) that, despite the dreaded traffic, she actually loved coming into the city each day. This was her chance to be with friends at lunch and after work. It was her social structure, her chance to be with people. She also missed lunches at local cafes, her favorite music that she listened to on her way to work, and other taken-for-granted simple pleasures. After a while, she began to feel trapped in her own home.

Other people crave power or fame. Only after they achieve it do they realize that the lack of any real privacy is a real drag. Instead of anonymity, which most of us take for granted, people are now looking over their shoulders. They are often exposed to more criticism and closer scrutiny.

I want to emphasize that I'm not taking a negative stance on any of these tradeoffs. Often, making more money is crucial, and outweighs any other consideration you might have. For many people, traffic is almost unbearable and would be worth avoiding at almost any price. Some people love the spotlight and the increased visibility. The important point here isn't the specifics, or any sort of value judgment, but the recognition of the relevance of asking yourself the important questions—"What am I really asking for, and why?"

When thinking about your job or career, it's important to consider what's right and good about your work in addition to focusing on what might be better. Feeling satisfied or being happy doesn't mean you aren't still working hard to make your career as successful as possible. You can have both—happiness and drive—without sacrificing your sanity.

Keep in mind that more responsibility might be a great thing, but it could very well lead to less personal freedom, privacy, and so forth. Similarly, a better paying position might make you feel more financially secure and it might be worth it—but you may give up other things that you haven't yet considered, or that you simply take for granted. It's all just food for thought. Remember, be careful what you ask for, because you might just get it—and more.

30.

ABSORB THE SPEED BUMPS
OF YOUR DAY

A metaphor I've found helpful in my own life is that of a speed bump. Rather than labeling the issues that come up during a typical work day as problems, I think of them as speed bumps. An actual speed bump, as you know, is a low bump in a road designed to get your attention and slow you down. Depending on how you approach and deal with the bump, it can be a miserable, uncomfortable, even damaging experience, or it can simply be a temporary slow down—no big deal.

If you step on the gas, speed up, and tighten the wheel, for example, you'll hit the bump with a loud thump! Your car may be damaged, you'll make a great deal of noise, and you can even injure yourself. In addition, you'll add unnecessary wear and tear to your car, and you'll look foolish and obnoxious to other people. If, however, you approach the bump softly and wisely, you'll be over it in no time. You'll suffer no adverse effects, and your car will be completely unaffected. Let's face it. Either way, you're likely to get over the bump. How you (and your car) feel once you get over it, however, is an entirely different issue.

If you ski or ride bikes, you already know how this works. If you tighten up your body, it's difficult to absorb the bump. Your form will be terrible and you may even fall. The bump will seem bigger than it really is.

Problems can be looked at in a similar light. You can be annoyed by them, think about how unfair and awful they are, complain about them and commiserate with others. You can remind yourself, over and over again, how difficult life is and how this problem is yet another justification for why you "have a right" to be upset! You can tighten up. Unfortunately, this is the way many people approach their problems.

When you think of your problems as speed bumps, however, they begin to look very different. You'll begin to expect a number of speed bumps to present themselves during a typical day. Like riding a bike, bumps are simply a part of the experience. You can fight and resist, or you can relax and accept. As a problem shows up during your day, you can begin to say to yourself, "Ah, here's another one." Then, like the ski mogul or bump on your bike ride, you begin to relax into it, thereby absorbing the shock, making it seem less significant. Then you can calmly decide what action or decision is likely to get you over this hurdle in the most effective, graceful manner. Like skiing, the calmer and more relaxed you remain, the easier it is to maneuver.

Thinking of problems as speed bumps encourages you to say things like, "I wonder what the best way to get through this one might be?" There is a healthy element of detachment involved, where you're looking at the problem objectively rather than reactively, looking for the path of least resistance. In other words, you assume there is an answer; you just need to find out what it is. This is in sharp contrast to seeing such concerns as problems, where it's tempting to think in terms of emergencies.

If you think about your work life, you'll probably agree that in one way or another, you do manage to get through a vast majority of the problems you are confronted with. If you didn't, you probably wouldn't last long in whatever it is you are doing. That being the case, where is the logic in panicking and in treating each problem like a major disaster?

My guess is that if you experiment with this one—simply thinking and labeling your problems as speed bumps instead of problems—you're going to be pleasantly surprised at how much more manageable your day is going to seem. After all, problems can be really tough, but almost anyone can maneuver over a speed bump.

31

HAVE A FAVORITE
BUSINESS CHARITY

Sometimes the best way to understand something of value is to study its absence. This is one of those times. Realistically, if you don't have a favorite business charity, how much of your business profit is going to go to charity? Five percent, two percent, zero? Who knows? We do know one thing for sure. In business, there's always going to be something to spend your money on. So, if you wait until everything else is taken care of, your business may never get around to giving.

Whether individually or through a business, there are so many good reasons to give to charity—need, satisfaction, compassion, desire to be of service, giving back, securing our future, embracing others, spiritual nourishment, and yes, even to get a tax deduction. Having a favorite business charity, however, provides you with even more reasons to give. It gives your business a service-oriented focus and goal. Rather than some abstraction or last-minute tax planning, you know exactly—month to month—how much money your business is sharing. It's quite satisfying. It's also an added incentive to do well. In other words, if your business pledges 5 percent of its net profits to charity, it means that the more money your business makes, the more money goes to those in need. This action makes your business a role model of how a company should operate. It makes you stand out because you're doing the right thing.

Whenever you stand out in a positive way, with sincere intentions, it can only come back to help you.

Having a favorite business charity has an intangible benefit to your business as well. It creates a feeling of team work, a coming together for a valuable accomplishment and a shared goal. It gives everyone involved in your business a feeling of satisfaction, the sense that your business is making a positive impact, not just for the employees, shareholders, and consumers, but for outside causes as well. It encourages people to think in terms of giving and sharing, which tends to make them do more of it outside the workplace as well. All of this good will and emphasis on sharing helps to create a more harmonious and gentle working environment. Giving makes everyone feel good about themselves and their efforts. This, in turn, helps people relax, maintain perspective, and stop sweating the small stuff.

If you own your own business, this strategy is easy to implement. You just start doing it. If you work for a small business, it can be relatively simple as well. You make your case to the owner or to the appropriate person. If you work for a large company, however, it can be a different story. In a large firm, there can be a silent assumption that "someone else will take care of it" or a feeling that no one would be willing to listen to your suggestion. And while that's a possibility, it's certainly worth a try. I've met a number of corporate leaders. My experience is that, for the most part, they're just like the rest of us. They have a heart and at least some degree of compassion. Most people enjoy giving. Don't make the mistake of assuming that your employer wouldn't be willing to have a favorite business charity. My guess is that most employers would love to contribute, and probably already do in other ways. Many would welcome this suggestion from you—even thank you. And if you give it your very best shot and you can't make it happen, that's okay too. You can implement a similar strategy in your personal life.

Can you imagine the cumulative impact on society if every small business and corporation would share 5 or 10 percent of their profits with those in need? Pretty amazing to think about it. Someday, as you look back on your career, you'll probably be proud of many things. If you participate in giving to charity, this will be near the top of your list. By encouraging your business to take action, to create a favorite business charity, you will have made an important contribution to the world. Thank you for doing your part.

32.

NEVER, EVER BACKSTAB

I was attending a corporate function prior to being a guest speaker when a young man approached me and introduced himself. He seemed nice enough until he launched into his backstabbing mode.

He moaned and complained about his boss and many other people he worked with. Within ten minutes, I became an expert on the "dirt" in his company. If I were to believe his version of the story, his entire firm was completely screwed up—except, of course, for himself.

The sad part of it was that I don't even think he was aware that he was doing it—it seemed to be a part of his ordinary conversation. Apparently, backstabbing was something that he was in the habit of doing.

Unfortunately, this man is not alone in this tendency. As someone who travels to diverse groups of people in different parts of the country, I'm sorry to report that backstabbing is alive and well. Perhaps one of the reasons it's so prevalent is that too few of us consider the consequences.

There are two very good reasons never again to backstab. First of all, it sounds terrible and makes you look really bad. When I hear someone slamming someone behind his back, it says nothing about the person they are referring to, but it does say a great deal about their own need to be judgmental. To me, someone who slams a person behind his back is disingenuous or two-faced. I doubt very much that the man I'm referring to in the above example said the things to his coworkers that he said to me. In other words, he would put on a smile and say nice things to them but, behind their backs, he would act in a completely different way. To me that's not fair play, and it's a poor reflection on oneself.

But aside from being a mean-spirited and unfair thing to do that makes you look bad, it's important to realize that backstabbing creates other problems for you as well. It causes stress, anxiety, and other negative feelings.

The next time you hear someone backstabbing someone else, try to imagine how the offending person actually feels—beneath the confident, secure appearance. How does it feel to say nasty, offensive, and negative things about someone else who isn't even there to defend themselves? Obviously, that's a loaded question—but the answer is so obvious that it's almost embarrassing to discuss. I know that when I have backstabbed in the past, my words have left me with an uncomfortable feeling. I remember asking myself the question, "How could you stoop so low?" You simply can't win. You may get a moment or two of relief from getting something off your chest, but you have to live with your words for the rest of the day—and longer.

Backstabbing also causes anxiety. The man I was talking to was sure to speak in a quiet voice—he didn't want to be heard. Wouldn't it be easier and less stressful to speak kindly about others, in a respectful tone? When you do, you don't have to worry whether or not someone will overhear your conversation or share your backstabbing stories with others—perhaps with the person you're attacking behind his back. Indeed, when you backstab, the pressure's on—you're on guard, now forced to protect your secret. It's not worth the price!

Finally, it's absolutely predictable that if you backstab someone, you will lose the respect and trust of the people you are sharing with. Remember, most of the people you're sharing with are your friends or colleagues. It's important to realize that, even if they appear to enjoy what you are saying, and even if they too are participating in the gossip, there will always be a part of them that knows that you are capable of backstabbing. They've seen it firsthand. It's inevitable that they will ask themselves the question, "If he will talk behind someone else's back, wouldn't he be capable of doing the same thing to me? What's more, they know that the answer is yes.

One of the nicest compliments I ever received was when someone with whom I have a great deal of contact said to me, "I've never heard you say a mean thing about anyone." Unfortunately, as I mentioned above, I have said mean things about others behind their backs, and I'm not proud of it. However, I took this compliment to heart because I'm doing my best to avoid backstabbing at all costs.

No one bats 100 percent. An occasional comment or the sharing of feelings probably isn't going to cause you great stress or ruin your reputation. But, all things being equal, it's a really good idea to put backstabbing out to pasture, forever.

33.

ACCEPT THE FACT THAT, EVERY ONCE IN A WHILE, YOU'RE GOING TO HAVE A REALLY BAD DAY

Recently, I had one of those bad days that, in retrospect, was absolutely hilarious. It seemed that everything that could go wrong did. Here are a few highlights: I was asked to fly to a different state to give a talk to a large group of people. To be honest, I really didn't want to go because I had just returned home from a series of trips and was missing my family a great deal. I was tired, jet-lagged, and behind in my work. Although I already had plans, I was informed by my publisher that this was a very important event and that the group would really appreciate my being there, so, I agreed to go.

On the way to the airport, I was caught in one of the worst traffic jams I've ever experienced—a normally forty-five-minute drive took well over two hours. I compounded the problem by spilling coffee all over my shirt.

When I arrived at the airport, the plane was late and my seat had been given to someone else, leaving me crammed in the middle seat. This is difficult for me because not only am I a very tall person who is claustrophobic, but I also do quite a bit of writing on airplanes. (In fact, I'm writing this strategy en route from Miami to San Francisco.) Because the plane was late, I missed my connection in Chicago and had to wait many hours to catch the last flight that evening. While I was reading in the Chicago airport, a woman tripped over someone's suitcase and spilled her sticky soft drink directly in my open briefcase. While she was apologizing, the rest of her drink spilled on my book! My speaking notes, ideas for this book, as well as my airline tickets, bills, photos of my children, and many other things were essentially ruined.

When I finally arrived at my destination, I was exhausted, but it was almost time to "wake up." So, with no sleep, I took a shower and went downstairs. My instructions were to meet my escort to the event in the hotel lobby at a certain time, but she never showed up! I called the convention center where I was to speak, and was informed that they wouldn't allow me in without my escort, due to some strange security issues they were having. I was told, once again, to stay where I was and to wait for my ride. You've probably guessed by now that I missed the event. Essentially, I "stood up" 2,000 people who were expecting me to speak. It was clearly "one of those days."

As is often the case, it really wasn't anyone's fault—just a comedy of errors, bad luck, and poor communication.

Disaster, right? An emergency? Time to panic? Hardly. The way I look at it is this: Why should I be exempt from the rest of the human race? Let's face it. We all have really bad days every once in a while. It must have been my turn. It had been a long time since I had experienced a work-related day like that. In fact, until that day, I'd never missed a scheduled speaking event for any reason. I guess it was inevitable.

This isn't a crass, apathetic, I-don't-care attitude. To the contrary, probably like you, I do my absolute best and often go to great lengths to ensure a punctual arrival. I take great pride in an almost perfect record of noncancellations of events and, when I do arrive, I do the very best I can to speak to the concerns of my audience. Yet we're all human. Beyond giving 100 percent, I don't know what can be done. Do you know something I don't?

I've found that it's helpful to accept the fact that every once in a while, it's going to happen to you too. It may not be a speaking engagement, but it will be something. This doesn't mean you like it; only that you make peace with this inevitable fact of life. This way, instead of being surprised and frustrated, wondering "how can this be happening to me," you can learn to make allowances in your attitude for this (hopefully) occasional nightmare. When you leave room in your heart for human error and tricks of nature, it allows you to keep your sense of humor, to not take yourself or your role too seriously, and to make the best of a bad situation. It also allows you to be forgiving of others who also make innocent mistakes on occasion and have bad days of their own.

As is usually the case, when you keep your cool instead of panicking, most everyone else will rise to the occasion as well. In this particular instance, I ended up spending the day with several truly delightful and talented people. We were able to salvage the meeting by doing a book-signing instead. Although we had obviously hoped for a different type of day, we made the best of the day we had, and ended up laughing together and having a lot of fun. The world didn't stop spinning simply because Richard Carlson had a mishap.

You can look at situations like this (and so many others) as horrible and frustrating—or you can look for a silver lining. And even if you can't find any silver linings, you can at least laugh at yourself and the way the universe sometimes works and make the best of it. My suggestion is simple: Accept the fact that every once in a while, you're going to have a really bad day. So what else is new?

34.

RECOGNIZE PATTERNS
OF BEHAVIOR

No matter where you work or what you do, becoming an expert in recognizing patterns of behavior can help you reduce the stress in your life by eliminating many of your unnecessary interpersonal conflicts. It will also help you to keep your perspective by being less surprised when "stuff happens." When you learn to recognize patterns of behavior, you'll be able to detect problems before they have a chance to get out of hand, nip certain arguments in the bud, and prevent hassles that might otherwise manifest themselves.

If you take a careful look at the people you work with, you'll probably agree that most people (you and I too) have a tendency to repeat patterns and engage in habitual reactions. In other words, we tend to be bothered by the same things, irritated by the same sets of circumstances, argue over the same sets of facts, and act defensively toward certain types of behavior. Indeed, for most of us, our reactions to life, particularly stress, are fairly predictable.

This being the case, it's enormously helpful to take careful note of the people you work with—and recognize any negative or destructive patterns of behavior that are likely to repeat themselves. You might notice, for example, that if you take on or challenge a member of your team, he will become defensive and tend to argue. This doesn't mean it's never appropriate to challenge him—there will certainly be times when it is. What it means is that when you recognize, with relative certainty, what's going to happen if you engage in certain types of interactions, you might determine that it's not worth getting into. In this way, you can avoid unnecessary conflict and spend your time and energy in more efficient ways. In order to be able to do this, of course, you'll have to take an honest look at your own patterns of behavior. Perhaps you're the one who starts some of the arguments, or you are a willing participant once they get going.

Maybe there is someone in your office who is virtually incapable of completing a project on time—he's always a day or two late. He's always got a great and legitimate-sounding excuse, yet the end result is always the same—he's late. By being aware of the pattern and the virtual certainty with which it occurs, you may be able to protect yourself, or at least be less frustrated by it. You can attempt to avoid participating in projects with him where on-time performance is a must. If working with him can't be avoided, you can try to build in some extra time, or get off to an early start, knowing full well what is likely to occur. And in a worst-case scenario, you will probably be less stressed out by his lateness because you already knew it was going to happen.

Perhaps someone else you work with gets argumentative when she feels criticized. If you recognize this particular pattern of behavior, you might think twice before offering habitual advice that she is likely to receive as criticism. Again, if it's necessary and appropriate to criticize or offer advice, that's a completely different story. What I'm referring to here is the daily, habitual types of comments that lead to hard feelings and unnecessary conflict.

Maybe a friend or coworker is someone who loves to gossip. By recognizing this pattern of behavior, you can avoid a great deal of potential grief and stop rumors before they have a chance to start. You begin to realize that if you share a story with her, she *is* going to share that story with others. It doesn't matter whether you ask her not to—or that she promises that she won't—or that her intentions are pure. This doesn't mean she's a bad person, only that her pattern is that she can't help but gossip. If you recognize the pattern, you have an enormous edge. You can bite your tongue and keep your secrets to yourself when you are with her, unless you really don't mind her sharing them with others. And if you make the decision to go ahead and tell her something, don't get upset when others discover your secret. It was predictable. It's part of the pattern.

I could go on and on. A person who is cheap is almost always cheap. Someone who gets jealous usually does so on a consistent basis. Someone else who steals the glory does so whenever the opportunity presents itself. A person who is dishonest tends to be dishonest whenever it seems to suit his needs. Someone who is hypersensitive will likely feel criticized, regardless of how gentle you attempt to be. An individual who is consistently late will probably show up late even though you've asked her not to—and so forth. Once you witness the pattern, whatever it is, it's a bit self-destructive to feed into it.

By recognizing patterns of behavior, you are in the driver's seat at work. This type of reflective wisdom allows you to better choose what to say and what not to say; who to spend time with and who to avoid, when possible. It helps you make the decision "not to go certain places" with certain people. Starting today, take a careful look at the patterns of behavior where you work. You'll be less stressed-out very soon.

35.

LOWER YOUR EXPECTATIONS

I was sharing this idea with a large group of people when someone in the back of the room raised his hand and said, "What kind of an optimist are you, suggesting that we lower our expectations?" His question was a valid one and, in fact, you might be wondering the same thing.

It's a delicate question to answer because, on one hand, you absolutely want to have high expectations and to expect that things will work out well. You want to believe that success is inevitable, and that your experiences will generally be positive. And with hard work and some really good luck, many (perhaps even most) of these expectations may indeed come true.

On the other hand, when you expect too much from life, when you are unrealisitc and demanding, you set yourself up for disappointment and a great deal of unnecessary grief. You'll probably also alienate at least some of the people you work with, because most people don't appreciate being held to unrealistic expectations. Your expectation is that the events in your life will evolve in a certain predictable way, and that people will behave according to your plans. When they don't, which is often the case, you end up stressed-out and miserable.

Often simply lowering your expectations, even slightly, can make your day (and your life) seem a whole lot easier. You can create an emotional environment for yourself whereby, when things do work out well, rather than taking them for granted, you'll be pleasantly surprised and grateful. And when your expectations don't go according to plan, it won't devastate you. Lowering your expectations helps to keep you from being so surprised when you bump into hassles and "stuff" to deal with. Instead of reacting negatively, you'll be able to say, "Oh well, I'll take care of it." Keeping your composure allows you to deal with the irritant or solve the problem, and be done with it.

Life just isn't neat and trouble-free. People make mistakes, and we all have bad days. Sometimes people are rude or insensitive. No job is entirely secure, and no matter how much money you make, it probably doesn't seem like enough. Phone lines and computers occasionally break down, along with everything else.

When I met Melissa, she worked for a software development company. She described it as her first "real job." She was young and driven, and had exceptionally high expectations. The problem was, many of her expectations weren't being met. She wasn't being treated with the degree of respect she wanted (or expected), and her ideas weren't being taken seriously. She felt under-appreciated and taken for granted. She was frustrated and burned-out.

I suggested she lower her expectations and consider thinking of her job in a new way. Rather than expecting her job to be all things to her, I asked if she might see it as a stepping stone to bigger and better things later on. She took the suggestion to heart, and her world began to change for the better. Without the mental distraction regarding what needs *weren't* being met, she was able to focus on the most essential aspects of her work. Her learning curve accelerated, and her stress level dropped.

About a year later, I received a nice voice mail message from Melissa letting me know how helpful it had been to lower her expectations.

Specifically she said, "I don't know why I made such a big deal about everything. Obviously, every job has tradeoffs to deal with. I guess I've learned to have a little more perspective and to take things in stride." She must have been doing something right, as she has been promoted twice since the last time I spoke to her.

Many people confuse expectations with standards of excellence. Please understand that I'm not suggesting that you lower your standards or accept poor performance as okay. Nor am I saying you shouldn't hold people accountable. What I'm referring to is making room in your heart for bad moods, mistakes, errors, and glitches. Instead of spending so much time being annoyed about the way things unfold, you will be able to take most of it in stride. Life and its many challenges won't get to you as much. This will conserve your energy and, ultimately, make you more productive.

Make no mistake: You'll still want to do everything possible to put the odds in your favor—work hard, plan ahead, do your part, be creative, prepare well, solicit the help of others, be a team player. However, no matter how hard you try, life still isn't always going to go as planned. One of the best ways to deal with this inevitability is to stop expecting it to be otherwise. So ease off your expectations a little, and see how much nicer your life can be. You won't be disappointed.

36

PAT YOURSELF
ON THE BACK

For most of us, there are times when we feel underappreciated, as if no one understands how hard we work and how much we are trying. One of my favorite pieces of advice has always been to praise often and tell people how much you appreciate them. You'll find bits of this advice scattered throughout this book. There are times, however, when no one seems to be applying that advice toward us, when no one seems to be appreciating us.

At times, it's important to stop what you are doing and pat yourself on the back. Take a few moments to reflect on what you've been doing and on the nature of your intentions and actions. Mentally review your accomplishments. Think about how hard you work and how much you are contributing to your goals, and to the people you are working with.

As simple as this sounds, it really helps! I've done this many times, and have found that it puts things in perspective. Sometimes it reminds me of how busy I have become, which gives me compassion for everyone else who is busy. I can recognize why people sometimes forget or are unable to be appreciative—they arc absorbed in their own work and their own lives.

Sometimes we get going so fast that we forget to pause and reflect. When we take a moment, however, we can regain our perspective and realize that we are making a valuable contribution to ourselves, our families, the people and business we work with, and humanity. Recognizing your contribution from within yourself is actually more powerful and satisfying than hearing it from others. In fact, in order to feel good about yourself and your efforts, you must be able to compliment yourself and recognize and acknowledge your contribution from within.

Almost everyone loves to be patted on the back by others. It feels good. However, when it's not happening, don't let it get you down or adversely affect your attitude. Praise from others is never a certainty, and making it a condition of your happiness is a really bad idea. What you can do is praise yourself and pat yourself on the back. Be honest and genuine regarding your compliments. If you're doing a good job, say so. If you're working long hours, give yourself some credit. If you're making life a little better for even one person, or making any type of contribution to society, then the world is a better place because of you. You deserve to be recognized. If you'll actually take the time to do so, I think you'll find this exercise is well worth the effort.

37.

BECOME LESS
SELF-ABSORBED

To me, there are very few human qualities less appealing than someone who is highly self-absorbed. A person who falls into this category takes him or herself extremely seriously. They love to listen to themselves speak, and value their own time—but no one else's. They are usually quite selfish with their time, love, and money, in addition to lacking compassion for those less fortunate. They are arrogant and come across as pompous and self-righteous. Self-absorbed individuals see others and often treat others as instruments or objects to get something they want. They usually see only one point of view—their own. They are right, and everyone else is wrong, unless, of course, you agree with them.

People who are self-absorbed can be rude, insensitive to the feelings of others, and primarily interested in themselves—their own wants, needs, and desires. They tend to see people in a hierarchical manner. In other words, they see certain people as being beneath them and, as such, they see them as less important than they are. Finally, self-absorbed people are poor listeners because, quite frankly, they aren't very interested in other people beyond a superficial level.

Obviously, I'm painting a worst-case scenario picture. Very few people are quite this bad. I paint this picture, however, because I believe it's important to be fully aware of what type of person you absolutely never, under any set of circumstances, want to become. This encourages you to be certain that none of these ugly characteristics ever creep into your life, and if they do, that you act quickly to move in a different direction.

Don't confuse self-esteem with self-absorption. The two are completely unrelated. In fact, you could say that the two are virtually opposite in nature. A person with high self-esteem loves others and feels good about herself. Because she already has what she needs in an emotional sense (feeling positive about herself), her natural instinct is to reach out to others in an unselfish way. She's extremely interested in hearing what other people have to say and in learning from them. She's very compassionate, always looking for ways to be of service or ways to be kind and generous. She is humble and treats everyone with respect and kindness.

There are many excellent reasons to become less self-absorbed. To begin with, as you can see by the picture I have painted, being self-absorbed is an ugly human quality. Beyond that, being self-absorbed is highly stressful. In fact, self-absorbed people sweat the small stuff as much, or more, than any other group of people—everything bothers or frustrates them. It seems that nothing is ever good enough.

For instance, self-absorbed people often have very poor learning curves. Since they don't listen well and aren't interested in other people, they don't have the advantage of learning from them. In addition, self-absorption comes across loud and clear to others, making them extremely resistant to wanting to be supportive or of any significant help. It's difficult to cheer on an arrogant person. In fact, it's tempting to want to see them fail.

For these reasons and so many more, it's a good idea to check in with yourself and make an honest assessment of your own level of self-absorption. Judge for yourself. If you feel you've drifted in that direction, then perhaps it's time to make a mental adjustment. If you do, everyone will benefit. You'll be more inspiring to others and, ultimately, you'll experience an easier and more fulfilled life.

38.

DON'T BE TRAPPED BY
GOLDEN HANDCUFFS

From the first time I heard the expression "golden handcuffs," it has had a profound impact on my perspective and on many of the lifestyle choices that I have made in my life. I've known a great number of people who have been trapped by these mental cuffs. My goal in writing this strategy is to see if I can help prevent this from happening to you or to someone you love or care about. Or, if you find you are already "cuffed," perhaps I can give you a nudge toward a potential solution.

The term "golden handcuffs" means that you voluntarily live at, or very close to the edge of your current means (or, in many cases, well above). It means that, in effect, you trap yourself into keeping a job or career (or moving in a career direction), and/or working too many hours because, while you may enjoy the benefits of, and completely rely on, a certain level of income, you may not enjoy (or you may even resent) what is required of you to earn that level of income. In other words, the rewards of your income are overshadowed by the stress of maintaining your lifestyle.

You may feel you don't have time for a life outside of work and wish that you could. Or, you may get precious little time to be with your friends, children, spouse, or other loved ones, or you may feel you spend too much time on the road as well as other difficult sacrifices. To have golden handcuffs means that you have knowingly or unknowingly chosen to trade certain aspects of the quality of your life (time, hobbies, relationships, solitude) in exchange for driving a certain type of car, living in a certain type of home, and enjoying certain material comforts and privileges. We get used to a certain lifestyle and can't imagine doing with less.

Pay particular attention to my use of the word "voluntarily" in my description of this problem. Obviously, this strategy doesn't apply to people who are living "on the edge" or barely surviving, spending every dollar earned on actual necessities. Instead, it applies in those instances where there is at least some degree of choice involved in your lifestyle. When you carefully and honestly examine your situation, you may find that you have more choices than you previously imagined. And, before you skip to the next strategy, read on! Because even if you're not trapped right now due to your current income, it's still important to be aware of this tendency so that you can avoid it later on in your career or if your circumstances change.

Some important questions to ask include: Did the seductive advertisement for that great new car convince you that you've "earned" the privilege of driving it? Are the high payments really worth it? Were those new clothes that were supposed to make you feel good about yourself worth working overtime to get? Is it really an honor to carry all those credit cards and, despite being able to purchase something practically anytime your heart desires, to be saddled with debt? Is a three-bedroom apartment that you can't quite afford really better than a two bedroom that is much less expensive? Might camping be as much fun as a hotel? Do the kids absolutely have to attend private school? Do you need two phone lines? Are restaurants always better than a bag lunch or a quiet picnic? Would taking public transportation or joining a car pool to work, thereby saving money on parking, gas, and road tolls, really be much of a sacrifice? Do you need so much stuff? Is more always better?

By most standards, Mark was a very successful businessman. He had been "climbing the corporate ladder" working for the same company for more than twenty years. He held an important, challenging position, enjoyed a large salary and benefits package, and was highly respected. He lived in a nice home, drove an expensive car, and his children went to a top private school. As the years went by, however, Mark became less interested in his career and longed to try something different. He loved nature and dreamed of a new career focused on helping the environment.

The problem was, Mark lived over his head. As he lost interest in his career, he found himself spending greater amounts of money in an attempt to fill up his empty feelings. He bought a new truck, an expensive boat and various other recreational toys. He rationalized his spending by assuming certain salary and bonus increases in future years. It got so bad that he was spending "future income" three and four years down the road. He had effectively trapped himself because in order to afford his lifestyle and continue to pay his ever-increasing bills, he was now forced to remain at the same job because of the relatively high salary. His options had disappeared and his dream would have to wait.

While it can be difficult to accept, there is, for many people, an effective way to deal with golden handcuffs. You can, in many cases, choose to lower your standard of living (that's right—lower), spend less money, consume less, and simplify your life. I know that this suggestion goes against the "American way" of ever-increasing wants and desires, and the seemingly universal tendency to want to increase our standard of living. Yet, if you think about it for a minute, this one simple suggestion could make your life much easier and less stressful.

I guess we all need to ask ourselves, are we really lowering our lifestyle if we are less stressed and worried? Would our standard of living be lessened if we were able to create more time for ourselves and for the people we love? Are we really worse off if we are genuinely easing our financial pressures and concerns, and perhaps even carving out a little more time to enjoy our lives?

I'm not arguing against achievement, material comforts, or the desire to improve the quality of your life. I believe in your right to be all you can be, and to have all that you deserve. I acknowledge that spending less money and living beneath your means can involve tough choices and trade-offs. Remember, however, that my goal in writing this book is to help you feel less stressed and to help you sweat the small stuff less often in your work life. One thing I am absolutely certain of is this: It's really difficult not to be sweating the small stuff if you are trapped by golden handcuffs.

I'm not suggesting that everyone who makes a good living needs to sell their home and move to a smaller home in the country; or that you should trade in your job that you've worked so hard for, in exchange for something less strenuous; or that you accept less income as a viable alternative. I am, however, suggesting that golden handcuffs can be a tremendous and painful source of stress and, if you take them off, your life can become a great deal easier. So, take a careful look at your lifestyle and decide for yourself if this strategy is for you. It can be difficult to face, but for many people, the freedom they will feel is well worth it.

39

GET REALLY COMFORTABLE
WITH USING VOICE MAIL

I always chuckle when someone says to me, "Gee, you leave really long voice mail messages." While it's true that I sometimes do so, it's a potentially stressful mistake to think of them as "long." The truth is, even the longest voice mail messages, if they are even remotely effective, are huge time-savers and excellent communication skills.

In most instances, the longest voice mail message you can leave is around three minutes. In those three minutes, you can leave very detailed, specific information, and respond carefully and accurately to specific questions or concerns, all the while allowing the other person the luxury of reflecting on your comments, hearing them several times, if necessary, and listening at their leisure. Voice mail messages are an excellent way to explain a point of view with the luxury of being uninterrupted. It's also a great chance for someone to listen to a message without familiar knee-jerk reactions such as defensiveness, or making a decision, or jumping to conclusions before hearing all the facts.

Obviously, I don't know your phone habits, but if they're anything like mine, it would be unheard of to have a personal phone call that lasts less than six or seven minutes, usually much longer. Most person-to-person calls include at least a few minutes of "How are you doing?" as well as other assorted distractions that are removed from the real bottom-line point of your call. I'd estimate that, even when my intention is to keep my conversation short, the average length of time per call is easily ten minutes.

As writing partners, my dear friend Benjamin and I put together four entire anthologies, including *Handbook for the Soul and Handbook for the Heart,* using voice mail more than 90 percent of the time. We live three hundred miles apart, and it was such an effective way of communicating that it made our job fun and easy. Since each of us had full-time jobs, we were able to leave thoughts and ideas on each other's voice mail during our breaks in the day. We would check our voice mail and/or leave messages at lunchtime, as well as early in the morning and late at night. We've discussed the issue many times and both agree that, had we chosen to communicate in person the bulk of the time rather than by voice mail, it's probable that none of the books would have ever been written. It simply would have been too difficult to coordinate our busy schedule and make the time for lengthy brain-storming sessions.

Some of you may think that by making this suggestion, I'm somehow unfriendly or don't enjoy personal conversations. Not true. As long as I have the time, and as long as the use of voice mail isn't more suited to the goals of my phone call, I love to talk to the people I work with. But see, that's part of the problem. Once I'm engaged in a conversation, I get so interested in what we're talking about that it's difficult for me to get off the phone. There are many times when a personal chat is preferred, and other times when voice mail is a perfect answer. And, certainly, I'm not suggesting that voice mail should replace any interactions you have regarding matters of the heart.

I'm not a voice mail salesperson and know it's not the perfect answer in all scenarios. It is, however, a real time-saver and an excellent way to communicate in certain situations. Many people already love voice mail and for you, this strategy may be a bit unnecessary. If that's the case, perhaps you can share this strategy with someone you feel it may benefit. But if you've had any sort of aversion to using voice mail, or if you're one of those people who complain about "long messages," I encourage you to rethink your position. By utilizing voice mail a little more often in your work-related calls, you can save tons of time and become even more effective in certain types of communication.

40.

STOP WISHING YOU WERE
SOMEWHERE ELSE

If you reflect on the insidious tendency to be wishing you were somewhere else, you may agree that it's a silly, even self-destructive thing to do. Before you jump up and say, "Wait a minute, I don't do that," let me explain what I mean.

There are many ways that we spend time wishing we were somewhere else. We'll be at work and wish we were home. Or during the middle of the week we might be wishing it were Friday. Sometimes we wish we were doing something else with our careers. We wish we had different responsibilities or could spend our time with different people. We wish our boss were different, or our employees. We wish our working environment were different or that we had a different kind of commute. We wish our industry were different, or that our competition would respond differently, or that our circumstances would change. This list could obviously go on. The problem is, these wishes aren't reality, but rather, they are thoughts of a different reality.

If you're not careful, you can begin to wish your life away, always wishing you were somewhere other than where you actually are. But you're not somewhere else. Rather, you're right here. This is reality. One of my favorite quotes is, "Life is what's happening while we're busy making other plans." A slightly different version might be, "Life is what's happening while we're wishing we were somewhere else." When you are wishing you were somewhere else, it's almost as though you are one step removed from life rather than actually being in it, open to life exactly as it is.

From a practical standpoint, it's very difficult to be focused and effective when your mind is preoccupied with where it would rather be. In fact, the two are a contradiction in terms. Your concentration suffers because there is a lack of engagement, a lack of zeroing in on what's truly significant. In addition, it's virtually impossible to enjoy yourself and what you are doing when you're focused more on where you'd rather be than where you actually are. Think about the things you enjoy most. In all cases, they are activities where you are completely absorbed in the moment, really focused on what you're doing. In the absence of the focus, the joy you experience is diminished. How much fun is it to read a good novel when you're thinking about something else?

But here's where this bit of wisdom gets a little tricky. When you're not getting any pleasure out of your work, it's easy to say, "Of course I'd rather be somewhere else, I'm not enjoying myself." But step back for a moment and take a closer look at what's contributing to the lack of enjoyment. The question is what comes first—a lack of enjoyment, or a mind that is focused elsewhere? Not all but at least some of the time, the boredom or lack of satisfaction we feel is caused not by our careers or by how we are spending our time, but by the lack of focus in our thinking. The fact that you're thinking about where you'd rather be is literally sapping the joy out of what you're doing.

I think you'll be pleasantly surprised, even shocked, if you make the decision to spend less time wishing you were somewhere else and more time focused on what you're actually doing. You may regain your spark and enthusiasm for your work, and in doing so, begin to have more fun. Plus, because you'll be more focused, you'll be more creative and productive as well.

Obviously, I'm not suggesting that it's not appropriate or important to plan for the future or dream. Nor am I saying you shouldn't make changes when you are drawn to do so. These are wonderful things to do and are very often appropriate. However, when you become more immersed in what you are doing instead of what you'd rather be doing, both the nature of your dreams as well as your planned course of action will begin to change. If you have a dream, the path to get there will become clear and obvious. Instead of being distracted by your conflicting and worried thoughts, you'll have a clear mind loaded with wisdom. Good luck on this one. I think you're going to find yourself enjoying your work more than you ever thought possible.

41.

ASK YOURSELF THE QUESTION, "AM I MAKING THE ABSOLUTE BEST OF THIS MOMENT?"

To me, one of the most important questions you can ask yourself is, "Am I making the absolute best of this moment?" Think about it. If you were to make the most of this particular moment, and then do the same in all future moments, life would have a magical way of working itself out. You would be effective and productive and, most important, it would be very difficult for things to bug you.

So often we spend our moments wishing they were different, complaining, whining, commiserating, or feeling sorry for ourselves. But when we get right down to it, spending our moments in this manner is not only a waste of time, it's absolutely counterproductive! By using this exercise, however, you may notice an almost immediate change.

Whenever you are feeling overwhelmed or stressed at work, ask yourself the question, "What am I doing with this moment?" Are you thinking about something stressful? Are you reminding yourself, once again, how incredibly busy you are? Are you justifying in your mind your "right to be upset"? Are you reinforcing a negative belief? Or are you using the present moment to its fullest advantage? Is your attitude and thinking pointed in a positive direction? Are you being solution-oriented?

I started practicing this strategy several years ago and have discovered something truly remarkable. It seems that in most instances when I'm feeling negative, overwhelmed, or pessimistic, I can improve my state of mind by checking in with this question. I guess I shouldn't be surprised that when I'm feeling overwhelmed, I'm spending my present moment thinking about all the things that I'm overwhelmed by, rather than spending it doing the best I can or coming up with the best plan of attack.

In reading this strategy, you can probably sense that when you don't make the absolute best out of this moment, you'll be a sitting duck to sweat the small stuff! You'll be thinking about all the things that bug you and all that's wrong with your life. Fortunately, the reverse is also true. When you're making the best of this moment, it's unlikely that you'll be sweating the small stuff because you'll be focused on solutions and enjoyment instead of problems and concerns.

42.

STOP SCRAMBLING

For many people, there are essentially only two speeds—fast and faster. It seems that, most of the time, we are scrambling around, moving very quickly, doing three or four things at once. Often we are only paying partial attention or half listening to the people we are working with. Our minds are cluttered and overly busy.

Perhaps the reason so many of us spend so much time scrambling is that we fear falling behind or losing our edge. Our competitors, and everyone else around us, seem to be moving so fast that we feel we must do the same.

It's important to note that, in this hyper, frenetic state of mind, our concentration suffers. We waste precious energy and have a tendency to make mistakes. When we're scrambling, it's difficult to determine what's truly most relevant because we are so preoccupied with getting everything done. Because we are moving so quickly, it's easy to get stressed out, nervous, and agitated. And because we are so "on edge," things get on our nerves easily and often. When we are scrambling, it's really easy to sweat the small stuff.

As an experiment, see if you can make a conscious effort to slow down—both your thinking and your actions. If you do, I think you'll be pleasantly surprised to discover that, despite the slower speed, you'll become more relaxed and far more effective. The reason this happens is that you'll regain your composure and be able to see the bigger picture.

Your stress level will drop dramatically and it will even seem like you have more time. Your thinking and listening skills will become sharper and more honed. You'll be able to anticipate problems rather than finding yourself in the middle of them so often.

I'd estimate that I operate at about half the speed I did ten years ago. However, I get about twice as much work accomplished! It's actually quite remarkable how much you can do when you're calm and collected. And perhaps even more importantly, you enjoy what you are doing far more than when you're rushing around. I fully acknowledge the need to be productive, and I realize how much work there is to do. However, ironic as it may seem, it's often the case that you'll get more done in less time when you stop scrambling so much.

43.

BECOME AWARE OF
YOUR WISDOM

I don't know anyone who questions the value of analytical thinking when it comes to being a success in whatever you do. But there is another type of intelligence, other than the use of your analytical mind, that is every bit as important—wisdom. Wisdom not only provides you with creative, appropriate ideas, perspective, common sense, and an excellent sense of direction, it also makes your life easier and less stressful. This is true because, unlike the use of your analytical mind which can be effortful and clouded by doubt, wisdom is derived from a sense of confidence, a sense of knowing which direction or course of action you should take, as well as a sense of inner confidence when making decisions, creating ideas, or solving a problem.

When you use your analytical mind, it's as if you are trying hard, actively pursuing your thinking. It requires effort. Analytical thinking involves filling your head with data, sorting, figuring, calculating, comparing, and wondering.

Wisdom, on the other hand, involves quieting or emptying the mind. When you access your wisdom, it's as if instead of actively pursuing your thoughts, you instead allow your thoughts to come to you. When wisdom is present, it's almost as though wise, clever and appropriate thoughts bubble up to the surface as if out of nowhere. Using your wisdom makes your life infinitely easier.

Have you ever struggled to find an answer? You think and think, rack your brain, and analyze the data. You go over and over the same sets of facts, yet nothing seems to happen. When you think in this manner, you often feel insecure, frightened, and quite stressed. You're easily bothered because you're trying so hard to figure everything out. You're trying hard, exerting effort, and tiring easily. There's a part of you that isn't sure you'll be able to find an answer. This is clearly a time when you have a tendency to sweat the small stuff.

Then for whatever reason you stop thinking—you quiet your mind— you forget about whatever is occupying your mind and, like magic, an answer appears. And not just any answer, a perfect answer! This is wisdom in action.

You can learn to access your wisdom by the simple recognition that often it's an appropriate use of the mind. You need to start trusting yourself enough to know that when you need an answer or an idea, quieting your mind—instead of filling it with data—may provide the best possible answer or solution. Accessing wisdom requires little more than the confidence in knowing that when you quiet your mind, your mind isn't turned off. Just like a back burner of a stove slowly cooking a pot of delicious home-made soup, your mind often works best when it's not operating at high speed.

Carol works as a property manager for a large apartment complex in Texas. It's her job to implement creative ideas to keep her existing tenants happy and to draw new prospective clients to the property. She shared with me her unique way of creating ideas. In her words, "Almost everyone in property management seems to think in exactly the same way—boring and predictable. I think it's because they think inside the box. I've discovered that it's better to think outside the box—to think differently. If I tell myself I want a new idea, however simple or weird it might be, the best thing I can do is clear my mind, stop trying so hard, and go jogging. Then, like magic, some idea will pop into my mind. Over the years I've had hundreds of simple, creative ideas that set my properties apart from the others. Little things that make a big difference; everything from our own community vegetable garden to our video checkout library. I've learned to trust my passive thinking as much or more than my analytical thought process. It's a lot more relaxing and more effective too."

I asked Carol how effective her ideas had been. She responded by saying, "I'm proud to say we have zero vacancy and a one-year waiting list."

The next time you find yourself mentally struggling, try quieting down your mind as a means of accessing your wisdom. You may be surprised at how quickly and easily the answer you need will come to you. With practice, you can learn to integrate wisdom into your daily life. It will be natural and effortless. Your wisdom is a powerful tool. Learn to trust it and, without question, you'll be a less-stressed and more effective person.

44.

REALIZE THE POWER
OF RAPPORT

Rapport is a subject that is often overlooked, yet it's critical to success. The ability to establish rapport contributes to a more relaxed way of being. It helps you establish trusting, long-term relationships based on mutual honesty and integrity. It helps you become a better "people person," a better negotiator, and an overall smarter and wiser businessperson. Rapport assists you in bringing out the best in yourself as well as in other people, and prevents others from acting defensively in your presence. In addition, the necessary ingredients of establishing rapport are identical to those that help you become a kinder, more patient, and relaxed person. So, you might think of establishing rapport as a form of self-therapy, a way to help you grow—personally, professionally, and spiritually.

Many of us have a tendency to dive in too quickly, push too hard, or ask for what we want from someone before we establish the necessary rapport. In most cases, this overzealous or ambitious attempt to get something from someone will backfire. It's a turn-off. You will have acted prematurely, and lack the vital connection necessary to optimize your goals.

When you lack a sense of rapport with someone, the problem can be difficult to describe. It may be that you lack a connection or a sense of trust. For whatever reason, you just don't click. Without rapport, you can come across as demanding, unrealistic, condescending, or arrogant. Sometimes you can't quite put your finger on what's wrong—but something is missing.

Many people do understand the need for rapport when they first meet someone. In other words, it's obvious that in order to sell someone something, or ask them to do something, it's necessary that they feel okay about you. The more subtle implication of rapport, however, exists after the first meeting. It's important to know that rapport is not necessarily something that you establish once and then lasts forever. Instead, it's necessary to reconnect with people on an ongoing basis, to check in with others to be sure you're in synch.

The best way to establish rapport with someone is to assume that you don't have it. In other words, don't take for granted that simply because you know someone or that because you've done business with them before, your rapport is intact. Instead, take the time to reconnect. Be more interested in listening than in speaking. Be highly respectful and courteous. Demonstrate your sincerity and your genuine concern. Ask questions and be patient. The key to rapport is to make the person you are with (or speaking to) feel as though he or she is the most important person in your life at that moment. You want to be so present with them—so genuine that they feel special. You can't fake this type of sincerity; you have to be real.

Dan assumed it was "a done deal." He had skillfully convinced his new client to purchase a large life insurance policy over the phone. Dan had never bothered with small talk with Walter, his client, but he had done his homework and knew his product well. There was no question in his mind that the product was in Walter's best interest. Walter knew that he was under-insured and had made the decision to purchase the policy. The two of them agreed to meet over lunch and sign the papers.

The moment they sat down, Dan pulled out the application and handed Walter a pen. Suddenly, something didn't feel quite right. Walter became uneasy, hesitant, and began to have second thoughts. Shortly thereafter, he stood up and announced to Dan that he was going to have to "think about it a little longer" before making his final decision. Needless to say, Dan lost the deal. He had minimized the power of rapport. Had he bothered to get to know Walter better, his client would have felt more comfortable with him and probably wouldn't have backed out.

Once genuine rapport is established, the rest of the interaction goes much more smoothly. I know people who, when I see them, somehow always take the time to reestablish their rapport with me. They ask me how I'm doing and actually wait to hear my answer before they go on or ask me to do something for them. They don't seem rushed or preoccupied with other things. Instead, they are right there with me, treating me as if I really mattered. These are the people I want to do business with. These are the people I want to be around.

If you take the time and energy to establish rapport with others, your life will begin to change immediately. You'll have a better connection with people, which will create more nourishing interactions—personally and professionally. You will be trusted, loved, and admired, and you will become far more effective when dealing with others.

45.

RECOVER QUICKLY

There's no question about it: There will be times when you make mistakes, sometimes big ones. There will be times when you overreact, offend someone, overlook the obvious, butt in when you're not wanted, slip up, say something you shouldn't have (put your foot in your mouth), and so forth. I've yet to meet a person who is exempt from these oh-so-human facts of life. So, perhaps the most important question isn't so much whether or not you will mess up, but rather how quickly you can recover when you do.

We can turn a relatively minor setback or mistake into a much bigger deal by overanalyzing our actions (or someone else's), or being too hard on ourselves. Or we say something wrong and can't let go of it, or we become defensive of our actions and refuse to apologize.

I remember an incident that occurred a few years ago where I was taking credit for something that, in retrospect, I could see didn't really belong to me. For whatever reason, I was acting more defensive and stubborn than I usually do. As a result, the person who felt slighted by me became angry and hurt. Other people became involved, and a great deal of energy was wasted. I was sharing my story with a friend of mine who said, "Richard, it seems to me you were really stealing her glory." He explained his rationale, which made a great deal of sense. I felt embarrassed and a little stupid. Later that day, I called the person to offer my sincere apology which, to my relief, was gratefully accepted. It turned out that all she really wanted was a simple acknowledgment for her actions and an apology from me. Had I done so earlier, recovered more quickly, a great deal of frustration and wasted energy could have been avoided.

That incident, and others like it, have helped me to learn how to recover from my mistakes much more quickly than before. There are still times that I overreact, get too defensive, fail to express my appreciation, say something I wish I hadn't, as well as many other day-to-day mistakes. The difference, however, seems to be that more often than not, I'm able to see my mistakes, admit to them, and move on—I recover quickly. The result seems to be that when someone I'm working with offers a suggestion, or some type of constructive criticism, rather than feeling defensive or struggling to point out how I'm right and they are wrong, I try to keep an open mind and remain receptive to growth. And you know what? In most cases, the person making the suggestion has at very least a grain of truth or some wisdom in their position. The trick seems to be the willingness to forgive yourself—and others—for being human and for making mistakes. Once you recognize the truth of the old adage, "To err is human, to forgive is divine," you create the emotional climate to recover from practically any mistake and move on.

I'm finding that by recovering more quickly, I'm learning from others as well as from my mistakes and, as a result, my work life has become substantially less stressful. If you reflect on this strategy, I'll bet the same can be true for you as well.

46.

ENCOURAGE COMPANY
STRESS-BUSTERS

Several years ago, I was speaking to a gentleman who was really upset that the company he worked for didn't do anything to relieve the stress in the office. He felt that the company executives were "selfish, uncaring people who didn't give a hoot about their overworked employees."

I asked the man, "If you were in charge, what changes would you make?" He had obviously given the matter quite some thought because he quickly responded by saying, "If it were up to me, I'd allow employees to dress casually and have shorter days on Fridays, I'd open a company gym, provide child care, and provide regular massages for everyone." "Wow," I replied, "that would be great. What did they say when you proposed these changes?" There was a long silence before he finally admitted that he had never so much as mentioned these ideas!

This person, like probably millions of other people, assumed that his employers knew that they should be doing these things. He also assumed the worst about the people running the show—that they were monsters and that they didn't care about the health and well-being of their employees. He was wrong.

I was touched by a phone call I received on my voice mail by the same man about six months later. He said that, after he made the request, he was shocked by the positive response. Several people, including his boss, had said to him, "Why didn't I think of that?" and "Great idea." He said that not all, but some of the ideas had actually been implemented, and that several ideas from other people were being seriously considered and looked into.

It's certainly not always true, but often it's the case that employers really do care about their people in the organization. It's also very often the case that the reason nothing is happening in the way of stress-reducing efforts is that no one is suggesting any changes. There is always plenty of complaining and wishing that things were different, but rarely someone who is willing to bring the ideas to the table in a logical, well-thought-out manner.

Even if you can't convince your employer to make any changes, it's often stress-reducing to hear their side of the story. The changes you'd like to see may be impossible, yet you might discover that there are people in your company—people just like you—who do care about your stress level and would like very much to do something about it. Knowing this is the case can be richly rewarding and can make you feel better about the company you work for. And in those rare instances when it appears that no one really does care, well, at least you can know that you did everything you possibly could to make a change.

I have a friend who works for a giant company in New York. She asked if it would be possible for her to work four days at home and continue to come into the office on Wednesdays so that she could move away from the city and spend more time with her son. The company agreed. She feels wonderful about the company she works with, and does an absolutely excellent job for them. Everyone wins.

Other companies, after being asked, implement casual Fridays, company work-out rooms, or other employee perks designed to make life around the office a little less stressful. A company I was familiar with many years ago had a bunch of vacation homes and would allow employees to sign up and use the homes at no charge. The same company had soft drink machines that didn't require the user to insert any money, and interesting guest speakers who would come and speak to the employees. I could go on and on.

Not all companies are open-minded, and you certainly wouldn't want to feel defeated if you can't pull it off, but it's almost always worth the effort to propose changes that would make employees feel less stressed. If enough people want the changes and if they are known to management and decision makers, who knows what may happen?

Keep in mind that happy employees who don't feel overstressed are usually more productive, less adversarial, and more loyal. They are also less likely to quit or feel bitter toward their employer than those who feel stressed-out and unappreciated. Sometimes if you can gently remind your employer of these facts, it really can make a difference. I hope it can happen for you.

47.

GIVE UP YOUR FEAR OF
SPEAKING TO GROUPS

I used to be absolutely petrified of speaking in front of any type of group. In fact, I was so scared that I actually fainted (twice) in high school while attempting to do so.

But I'm not alone. I've heard that public speaking is the number one fear in America. It seems that speaking to groups is even more frightening to people than air travel, bankruptcy, even death!

Just for fun, I ran this strategy by a respected friend of mine to see whether or not he understood why I would include this specific strategy in a book on becoming less stressed at work. His specific response was, "I know that speaking in public is a huge fear, but how would becoming less frightened to do so help you sweat the small stuff less at work?"

It's a fair question, but I have the answer.

A fear as big as this one doesn't exist in a vacuum. In other words, it doesn't show up only on those occasions when you are called on to speak in front of a group. Instead, the stress associated with speaking in front of others looms over you, perhaps very subtly, if there is any chance whatsoever that you will ever need to speak in front of people. Whether you may be required to give a presentation, a sales pitch, the results of a report or study, an all-out speech, or simply share an idea with others, the stress factor is the same—enormous—if you're scared.

Another factor to consider is this: If you're frightened of speaking to groups, even a little bit, you may avoid doing things that could greatly benefit your career, give you a promotion or more responsibility, or an advancement of some kind. Before I overcame my fear of speaking, I remember making many decisions based on the likelihood that I may or may not have to speak. Getting over this fear helped me to relax about my work so that I could focus on other things. It made my work life easier and far less stressful. There is no question that overcoming this fear has also helped me to become more successful as an author. Had I not done so, I doubt very much that I would be writing books, because writing books requires promoting them, often in front of huge groups of people.

If you have any fear whatsoever, I urge you to consider this suggestion very carefully. Once you get over the fear you experience, you will be less stressed and more easygoing in your work life. This will help you be more creative and solution-oriented because the distraction of this fear will be gone forever. Because you'll be less on edge, you'll be sweating the small stuff less and less.

The way to get over this fear is to put yourself in situations where you are required to speak to groups. You can start really small—even one or two others is a great place to start. There are classes you can take, coaches who can help you, books to read, and tapes to listen to. There are a variety of methods and strategies to look into. In the end, however, you'll have to take the first step and get in front of people. If you do, I think you'll find, as I have, that if you get over this common fear, you'll be richly rewarded in terms of the quality of your work and, indeed, the quality of your life.

48.

AVOID COMMENTS THAT ARE LIKELY TO LEAD TO GOSSIP OR UNWANTED CHATTER

This is a real eye-opener strategy that has helped me a great deal in my own life. It's proven to be a real time-saver, and has helped me to see how often I innocently contribute to my own stress.

If you're like most people, there are times when you make innocent, fairly benign comments to others about a variety of things. You'll say things like, "Did you hear about John?", "Have you heard about so and so?", or "Did you know that?" Sometimes you initiate the conversation. Other times you keep a conversation going without realizing that you're doing so. You'll embellish someone else's comments, share a story or example, get into too much detail, or ask one too many questions. Then, if you're like me, you'll wonder why you spend so much time on the phone and why you can't seem to get enough work done.

On the surface, this may not seem like a really big deal until you consider how much time and energy you spend engaged in conversations that may not be entirely relevant, or may not be happening at an ideal time. Think about how often you feel stressed for time or energy. How often do you look back on your day and wish you could have had just thirty more minutes to get something done or simply catch up? Or think about how often you're in a hurry to complete something.

If you take a careful look at how you actually spend your time, you may come to the same conclusion that I did: that there are many instances when I'm engaged in unimportant conversations, in person or on the phone, when I honestly don't have the time or energy to be doing so. As you might suspect, this tendency can contribute to your overall feelings of stress at work. This habit can leave you unnecessarily short of time, or force you to be in a constant rush. Unless you become aware of this tendency, it's easy to blame the world and the people you talk to during the day for your feeling overwhelmed, when in fact, you may have played a significant role in the problem.

Obviously there are many times when you want to be engaged in conversation with friends or coworkers, and that's perfectly fine and healthy. The trick is to be aware of when you are conversing out of habit rather than by choice. The slightest shift in your awareness in this tendency can pay tremendous dividends in the quality of your work life.

I used to think that all the time I spent talking about other people and discussing somewhat trivial things was entirely beyond my control. What I have learned is that this is only partially true. The truth is, only some of it is beyond my control. The rest of it, I have learned, I create all by myself with my own innocent comments and questions. I have learned that it's possible to shorten my conversations while remaining polite and respectful. I've also learned to avoid asking certain types of questions that I know are likely to lead to lengthy or unnecessary conversation unless I truly want to be talking *and* I have the time. The results have been spectacular. Even though I'm busier than ever before, I feel like I have even more time. What's more, when I do take the time to converse with others, I do so knowing that it's a good time to be talking.

This is a very powerful strategy because even if you add only an hour or so a week to your work life by virtue of biting your tongue, that's one extra hour of much-needed time that you didn't have before. That one hour can sometimes make the difference between a stressful week and a peaceful one. I'm not suggesting you become antisocial or rude, only that you be careful of what and how much you say—when what you say is likely to lead to further, perhaps unwanted conversation. You'll be amazed at the power of this strategy.

49.

SEE BEYOND THE ROLES

It's almost inevitable that you will (at least on occasion), have a tendency to see people as their role instead of remembering the person behind the role. In other words, it's tempting to forget that a businessperson (or anyone performing a job or a task)—whatever he or she happens to do—isn't really a businessperson, but a special, unique human being who happens to be doing business (or performing a task) in some capacity. A baker has a life of her own, her own stories and dramas to deal with. The flight attendant is tired and can't wait to get home. The person pumping your gasoline has a family, insecurities, and problems of his own. The corporate executive probably argues with her husband and has plenty of problems unknown to the rest of us. Your secretary loves her friends and children as much as you do, and feels the same frustrations as everyone else. Whether it's your staff or your boss, it's all the same. We're all in this together.

This problem of seeing others as their role is reinforced in so many ways. How often is our first question, "What do you do?" Or how often do we describe someone as "an accountant," or "a lawyer," as if the role is really who that person is? Some of this is probably inevitable, but we can, if we choose, begin to shift the way we see and label others and in doing so make our life so much more pleasant.

I recently heard a story about a woman's boss who was so locked into roles that he actually put his pencils in his out-box for his secretary to sharpen! It would have taken him a few seconds to do it himself, but in his mind it was her role and "By God, she was going to do it." He was either oblivious, or simply didn't care how this made her feel.

When you see people as human beings first—their role second—the people you are in contact with sense your deeper perspective. In other words, they see you in a different light as well. They often treat you better, listen to you, and make allowances for you that others don't enjoy. When you see beyond the roles that people perform, you also open the door for much richer, nourishing, and more genuine interactions. You get to know people, those close to you and those you merely come into contact with. People will like you and trust you. They will often go to great lengths to help you. Time and time again, people in stores, airports, and taxis have been super helpful to me simply because I treated them as a human being first.

My guess is, had the man in my above example treated his secretary more as a fellow person and less as her role, she would have probably sharpened the silly pencils anyway. As it was, however, the way he handled it made her feel like dirt and she ended up quitting the job. Sadly, she had been an excellent secretary. One small consolation was that the boss later realized how badly he had treated her. Hopefully, he learned his lesson.

One of the places I shop has some of the warmest, friendliest people I've ever met. Yet to this day, I often observe other customers treating them almost like objects—not really mean or disrespectful, but like they weren't even there, as if there isn't a person behind the counter who smiles and enjoys their children and their time off just like everyone else. As if he or she is a checker and *only* a checker, put here on earth to serve them and take their money. I observe people moving through the line, never looking up, never smiling, never saying hello. You've probably seen the same dynamic at your local store, as well as in restaurants, airports, taxis, buses, hotels, retail outlets, and every other place you can imagine.

This strategy is simple and easy to put into practice. You don't have to become best friends or even social with everyone you meet, or for that matter, anyone you meet or work with. It's not about that. Neither do you have to forget that roles are a part of life. If someone works for you, obviously it's appropriate that they treat you in a certain way.

My suggestion is simply to remember that each person is special, and is so much more than what they do. Each person you meet has feelings—sadness, joy, fears, and all the rest. Simply knowing this and keeping it in mind can transform your life in some simple yet powerful ways. You can brighten other people's days merely by smiling and making eye contact. You can contribute to making the world a nicer, friendlier place for others and for yourself.

50.

AVOID THE TENDENCY TO PUT
A COST ON PERSONAL THINGS

One of the stressful habits that many of us get into at work is that we tend to put a cost on too many things. In other words, we calculate in our minds the cost of what we are doing or owning—when we could be doing or owning something else. Obviously, there are times when this is enormously helpful, such as when we spend time watching television or organizing our desk when we could be spending that same time working on the report that is due tomorrow morning. In this case, it might be helpful to remind yourself that, in effect, that television program is carrying with it an enormous cost—perhaps even your job.

I remember when Kris and I bought a one-fifth interest in a sailboat. The only problem was that during the next two years we only stepped on that boat once—and even then it was for a picnic with our best friends, not for a sail. In this case, it was helpful for Kris and me to realize that our picnic had, in effect, cost us over two thousand dollars! Oh well, at least we had a lot of fun on the picnic.

There are other times, however, when it's important that we not put a price tag on what we are doing. I've known quite a number of people, for example, who rarely take days off to spend time relaxing or doing something just for fun because the "cost is too high." They make the mistake of calculating what they could be earning during the days, or even hours, they are away. Even on those rare occasions when they do get away, they find it difficult to relax because they are so preoccupied with what they could be doing instead, or with what they might be missing. They will say or think things like, "If I were seeing clients (or earning) at a rate of fifty dollars an hour, I could be making four hundred dollars today. I shouldn't be here." And while they are technically correct in their arithmetic, they are effectively eliminating any possibility for a calm, inwardly rich life—because in order to achieve a less-stressed life, you must value and prioritize your need for recreation, fun, quiet, and family at least some of the time. So, even if your earning capacity is much less than the above example, there still has to be some limit on how out-of-balance you allow yourself to become.

One of my fondest memories growing up was one day that my dad helped me move from one apartment to another. It was during the week, and my dad simply took the day off. Looking back, it was a time when my father was busier than ever before. He was running a giant company and was dealing with some very complex issues. His time was extremely in demand and valuable. I remember thinking I was being financially clever when I said to him, "Dad, this is probably the costliest move ever made," referring to the fact that he could have easily hired a few people to help me at a tiny fraction of the actual cost of his being there with me. Doing so would have been far less stressful, much cheaper, and a lot easier on his back. Without even thinking about it he looked at me and said, "Rich, you can't put a price tag on spending time with your son. There's nothing in the world I'd rather be doing than spending time with you." Those words have stuck with me for almost twenty years, and will do so for the rest of my life. I probably don't have to tell you that my dad's comment meant more to me that all of the thousands of hours he spent in the office "for his family." It made me feel special, important, and valued. It also reminded him that his life was more than "another stressful day at the office."

If you want to reduce the stress in your life and be a happier person, I have found it to be useful to look at certain issues without attaching a price to them—spending time alone, with someone you love, or with your children. When you take time doing things that nourish you, or spending time with people you love, it reduces the stress you feel in all aspects of your life, including work. When you know that, no matter what, certain parts of your life simply aren't for sale—at any price—it reminds you that your life is precious and, furthermore, it belongs to you.

Go ahead and allow yourself to do some things just for you. Take some time for yourself—take a regular walk, visit nature, read more books, learn to meditate, get a massage, listen to music, go camping, spend more time with your loved ones or alone—but do something. And when you do, don't spend your time thinking about how you could be more productive. My guess is that if you learn to value your personal life and your true priorities, you'll discover that life will seem easier than before. You'll be surprised by the number of good ideas that will pop into your mind when you allow yourself to have fun—without calculating the cost.

51.

WHEN YOU SOLICIT ADVICE,
CONSIDER TAKING IT

One of the most interesting interpersonal dynamics that I've been able to observe is the tendency that many people have to share something that is bothering them, yet completely ignore the advice they receive in response. The reason I find this so interesting is because, as I have listened to conversations over the years, I've been impressed over and over again by a great deal of the creative advice I have heard. So often, it would appear as though the advice being given would solve the problem at hand, easily and quickly. In fact, there have been plenty of times that I've heard ideas designed for other people that were completely dismissed by the person to whom it was intended—that I've taken as a means of improving my life!

Obviously, there are times when we share a concern simply because we want to vent or because we simply want someone to listen to us. But there are other times when we are genuinely confused about what to do and actively seek advice, such as when we say, "I wish I knew what to do," or "Do you have any ideas?" Yet when a friend, spouse, coworker, or someone else offers a suggestion, our immediate response is to tune it out, or in some way dismiss it.

I don't know exactly why so many of us tend to dismiss the advice we receive. Perhaps we are embarrassed that we need help or we hear things we don't want to hear. Maybe we are too proud to admit that a friend or family member knows something we don't. Sometimes the advice we receive requires effort or a change in lifestyle. There are probably many other factors as well.

I'm the first to admit that I do many things wrong. But one of the qualities I'm most proud of—and am certain has helped me a great deal in both my personal and professional life—is my ability to really listen to advice, and in many instances, take it. I'm absolutely willing to admit that I don't have all the answers I need to make my life as effective and peaceful as possible. Usually, however, someone else can offer a suggestion that can help me. Not only do I often benefit from the advice I receive, but the person offering it to me is thrilled that I'm actually willing to listen and even *take* the advice. People have suggested that I talk too much—and they were right. I've been told I needed to become a better listener—and I did. People have suggested that I take a certain course or try a certain diet, and I have. And it really helped. Over and over again, I've asked people to share with me any blind spots they see in my attitude or behavior. As long as I remain receptive and nondefensive, I can almost always learn something. And sometimes, one simple suggestion can make a world of difference.

The trick is to be willing to admit that other people can see things about us (or our circumstances) that we may be too close to or too personally involved with to see ourselves. So, while you probably won't want to accept all the advice that comes your way, you may want to become just a little more open to some of it. My guess is, if you do, your life is going to be a whole lot easier.

52.

TAKE ADVANTAGE OF
YOUR COMMUTE

I was talking to an executive of a fairly large corporation who was complaining to me about his "nasty commute," which took almost an hour and a half each way. "Wow," I said, "that's too bad, but at least you're able to read some good books." His response shocked me. He said in a dead serious tone, "What are you talking about? I don't have any time to read." At first I thought he was kidding. Once I realized he wasn't, I said, "You mean you don't listen to audio tapes of books while you're in the car?" He shook his head no. "What do you do for those three hours each day?" His answer was a little uncertain; he didn't seem to really know how his commuting time was spent. I gather that he spent those three hours a day being mad at the traffic and feeling sorry for himself. I'm sure he spent a little time listening to the news and perhaps making a few phone calls on his cell phone, but for the most part, he just sat there wishing things were different. Keep in mind that this is a highly educated, extremely successful businessman. I wonder what he would think about any of his employees who wasted three hours a day, without even knowing what they were doing.

Assuming he works fifty weeks a year, he spends 750 hours a year driving to and from work. That's a staggering amount of time for anyone to waste, especially when there is such a great alternative.

Not all, but many great books are now available on audio tape. If your commute is long enough, you can listen to the entire book while driving to and from work. You can see how incredibly valuable your driving commute time can be, should you decide to look at it that way. I love audio books. With two small children, a hectic work schedule, lots of travel, and a ton of outside interests, I don't have nearly the time to read that I wish I did. But audio tapes have solved that problem. My daily commute isn't very long, but I do take advantage of the time I have to drive, as well as the traffic jams I get stuck in. Living in the San Francisco Bay Area, I get plenty of them! During these times, I listen to all sorts of great books—novels, self-help, and all the rest.

If you're one of the millions of people who must commute to work or who regularly gets stuck in traffic, rejoice! You now know of a way to take advantage of that commute. (And if you take a bus or train, you can either listen to audio books or read a book.) You might even want to start an "audio book club" with some of your friends. Four or five of you could purchase a few tapes and take turns listening to them. You'll get hours of listening enjoyment for very little cost. Give it a try. When you get home from work, instead of complaining about your commute, you'll be able to discuss the latest book you've listened to.

53.

LET GO OF BATTLES
THAT CANNOT BE WON

One of the major contributing factors to self-created stress is the tendency that most of us have to hold on to battles that we have virtually no chance of winning. For whatever reason, we keep alive unnecessary arguments and conflicts, we insist on being right, or we try to get someone to change when there is almost no possibility that we will succeed. We bump up against stone walls, but instead of backing off and taking the path of least resistance, we keep right on struggling.

Suppose you're driving to work when some aggressive driver starts to tailgate you. You get annoyed and bothered. You focus your attention in the mirror. If you get mad enough, you might even slow down or tap your brakes just to retaliate. You think to yourself how awful the world has become and how road rage is a sad fact of life.

Even though your assessment of this driver may be correct, this is clearly a battle that you cannot win. By participating in the battle, the best that can happen is that you'll end up frustrated. At worst, you may even contribute to the cause of an accident. It's not worth it because either way you lose. By recognizing that this is a battle not worth fighting, you can calmly move to a different lane and allow the driver to go on and have his accident somewhere else. Period, end of subject. Let go of it, and go on with your day.

An arrogant and chauvinistic male CPA was arguing with two bright female colleagues. They were questioning his conclusion regarding a complex tax issue, and he wasn't interested in listening. They provided what appeared to be conclusive proof of their position, including supportive documentation and precedence. Despite his lack of evidence to support his position, he brushed them off and discounted their data. Officially, he was the decision maker and, as far as he was concerned, the case was closed.

The fact of the matter was, in this instance, *his* reputation was officially on the line, not theirs. They were trying to do him a favor and save him the embarrassment of a mistake and the hassle of correcting it later on down the road. Furthermore, his error wasn't intentional, nor was it significant. The truth was, they had done everything they could do. It was clear that this was a battle they were not going to win—there was nothing they could do to change his mind. They could spend the next week complaining to each other and feeling frustrated—or they could let it go and stay focused on their own integrity and excellent work.

Luckily, the two women had learned not to become overly dramatic over relatively small things. You might say they had learned not to sweat the small stuff—which this clearly was an example of. Keep in mind that, had the stakes been higher, or had the issue involved integrity or a significant amount of money, they may have decided to take their efforts to a new level. But, in this instance, it clearly wasn't worth the hassle. Their decision had nothing to do with apathy; both women were real pros. It was simply a matter of having the wisdom to know how to choose their battles carefully.

Obviously, if something legitimate or terribly important is at stake, you may have to prove your position and it will be worth the trouble. Most of the time, however, that's not where daily frustration stems from. In fact, most of us handle the "big stuff" pretty well. The stress you feel often comes from fighting those "no chance of winning" battles where the outcome is practically irrelevant anyway.

Perhaps you're frustrated by the complaining of a coworker. You may spend countless hours and a great deal of energy attempting to share with her why she shouldn't be so upset. But try as you might, she just keeps on complaining. For every valuable insight you share with her, she comes back with yet another, "Yeah, but . . ." and never, ever takes your advice. If you're frustrated by this type of typical interaction, it's because you're fighting a battle that can't be won. She's probably going to be complaining for the rest of her life. Your involvement, caring, ideas, and insights have zero effect. Does this mean you should stop caring? Of course not. It simply means you can dismiss the idea that you are ever going to convince her to stop complaining. Case closed. You can wish her well and be there for her as a friend, but if you want less stress in your life you're going to have to let go of the battle.

We fight these silly battles (and so many others) sometimes out of stubbornness or out of our own need to prove ourselves, other times out of pure habit, and sometimes simply because we haven't thought through exactly what it is we are hoping to accomplish or where our efforts are likely to lead. Whatever the reason, however, this tendency is a serious mistake if your goal is to stop sweating the small stuff. The great football coach Vince Lombardi was known to have said, "When you're doing something wrong, doing it more intensely isn't going to help." I couldn't say it any better.

I'm certain that one of the major reasons I'm a happy person is that I'm usually able to differentiate between a battle worth fighting and one that is better left alone. I've always felt that my personal sense of well-being is far more important than any need I might have to prove myself or participate in an irrelevant argument. That way I can save my love and energy for truly important things. I hope you'll take this strategy to heart because I know it can help you stop sweating the small stuff at work.

54.

THINK OF STRESS AND
FRUSTRATION AS DISTRACTIONS
TO YOUR SUCCESS

I couldn't tell you how often I've been asked the question, "Don't you think you need to be stressed and harried to be successful?" I've yet to meet anyone who can convince me that the answer to this question is "Yes."

Many people assume that stress and success are linked in the same way that glue sticks to paper. The assumption is, "There's a huge price to pay in order to achieve your dreams, and enormous stress is an inevitable and essential part of the process." People think of their stress as a source of motivation. Consequently, people are not only looking for verification of stress in their work life, but even more to the point, they begin to assume that stress is a valuable emotion to have, something they actually need to stay motivated and to keep their edge. Thus, they begin to look and behave in very stressful ways—they become short-tempered and poor listeners. They don't allow adequate time between appointments, therefore assuring the need to scramble and feel rushed. They become nervous and agitated. They lose their perspective and wisdom. They rush out the door in the morning and complain about how busy they are when they finally return home after work. In short, they sweat the small stuff—big time!

The problem is, if you assume that stress is a positive and necessary factor, you're going to create—knowingly or unknowingly—a great deal more of it. If, however, you can begin to think of stress as a distraction that is actually interfering with your goals and dreams, you can begin to rid yourself of a great deal of it.

Stress is, in fact, a distraction. It interferes with clear and logical thinking. It makes wisdom, insights, and creativity more difficult to bring forth. Stress is also exhausting, robbing you of valuable and precious energy—both physical and emotional. Finally, stress is an enormous source of relationship problems. The more stressed-out you are, the more quick-tempered you become. You lose your ability to stay focused, and your listening skills are affected. You lose your compassion and sense of humor.

I acknowledge that some degree of stress is inevitable. And certainly, becoming successful in whatever you do can be difficult and demanding. However, thinking of stress as valuable makes matters worse, not better. Looked at in this way, it's easy to see that stress isn't something you want to think of in a positive light. Far from being your primary source of motivation, stress has a way of defeating your spirit and energy. And contrary to the notion that stress helps you keep your edge, it actually gives that edge to your competitors.

My suggestion is this: When you begin sweating the small stuff at work, and when you begin to feel stressed-out, gently remind yourself that, while work may be difficult, the stressful feelings you are experiencing aren't helping and certainly aren't worth defending. In doing so, you may begin to notice the some of the stress that you've always assumed was necessary will begin to fade away. If so, you'll experience the success that comes from seeing stress as a distraction, instead of as an ally.

55.

ACCEPT THE FACT THAT THERE'S ALMOST ALWAYS GOING TO BE SOMEONE MAD AT YOU

This is a difficult concept to accept, particularly if, like me, you are a "people pleaser," or worse still, an approval seeker. Yet I've found that if you don't make peace with this virtual inevitability, it guarantees that you will spend a great deal of time struggling with one of the unfortunate realities of life—disappointment.

The fact that someone is virtually always going to be mad or at least disappointed in you is inevitable because while you're busy trying to please one person, you're often disappointing someone else. Even if your intentions are entirely pure and positive, you simply can't be in two places at one time. So, if two or more people want, need or expect something from you—and you can't do it all—someone is going to be left disappointed. When you have dozens, even hundreds of demands on your time, and requests being fired at you from all different directions, a certain number of balls are going to be dropped. Mistakes are going to be made.

Your boss or client needs you to do something—the only problem is, your child or spouse needs you too at the same time. You're a waitress at a busy restaurant and every table seems anxious—you're doing the very best you can, but customers are still mad. Four people asked you to call them before five o'clock. Whoops, the second call took much longer than anticipated. The two who didn't receive calls are probably going to be upset. If you hurried the call you were on, you risked upsetting that person. Either way, someone's left upset. Or you go the extra mile to do an excellent job on one project—but only have time to do an adequate job on another project. Again, you let someone down. You forget someone's birthday. Even though you remembered nineteen other birthdays, you still managed to upset one person. And so it goes.

You can try and try—you can put all the odds in your favor, you can make allowances for contingencies and mix-ups, but there are still going to be errors. And when errors happen, or when you prove that you're human; when you're overcommitted, need some time to yourself, forget a promise, meeting, or commitment; then someone is going to be hurt, upset, mad, or disappointed. In my heart, I know that I try as hard as any human being can try—and I can tell you there is no way around it (at least I haven't found one)! Here's a personal example.

For a period of time, I was blessed in receiving in excess of three hundred letters a week from readers. A good number of these letters asked for a personal response, and in my view, each person deserved one. After all, someone who takes their time and effort to write a kind letter is, to me, quite special. To this day, I appreciate every letter I have ever received—many bring tears to my eyes. But it can also be frustrating because like almost everyone else, my problem is that there are only so many hours in a day and, again like everyone else, I have to juggle many different responsibilities and commitments.

I have a hectic travel schedule and tight writing deadlines. I have numerous speaking engagements to prepare and deliver on an ongoing basis, promotional commitments, and dozens of other requests for my time each and every day. Most importantly, I have a family that I love very much and wish to spend time with, as well as a few close friends.

To put it in perspective, if I were to spend even ten minutes apiece on all the letters I receive, it would take virtually all of my time. In any event, you certainly wouldn't be reading this book today because there would have been no time to write it. What can I do? I hired a responsive person to help me answer my mail. Each week, she helps me choose as many letters as possible to answer personally, and she responds to the rest. Her letters are kind, thoughtful, and respectful. For a while, I thought I had solved my dilemma.

Not! Although a vast majority of people understand my predicament, there is always a small percentage of people who are disappointed, and a few who are enraged that I didn't have the courtesy to write them myself. Again, the problem is you really can't please everyone, no matter how hard you try. It's no different for me than it is for you.

When you make peace with this fact of life, a huge weight is lifted off your shoulders. Obviously you would never intentionally hurt or disappoint someone. In fact, most of us will do everything within our power not to— yet it's still going to happen. And when you know it's inevitable, your gut reaction to the disappointment is going to be much more peaceful. Rather than becoming upset, defensive, or guilty, you'll maintain your bearings and remain compassionate. You'll understand that there's simply nothing you can do—other than your best. You didn't intend for it to happen, you did everything you knew how to prevent it, yet it happened. And it will happen again. It's time to let it go. And in letting go, you will find peace.

56.

DON'T LET YOUR OWN THOUGHTS
STRESS YOU OUT

I'm often asked the question, "What is the single most important thing a person can do to stop sweating the small stuff?" I must confess that I do not know for sure what that single secret would be. I can tell you, however, that way up there on my list would be my suggestion of not allowing your own thoughts to stress you out.

Think about how often we all have conversations in the privacy of our own minds. It happens, practically nonstop, all day long, every day of our lives. We're in the car thinking about something—a deadline, an argument, a potential conflict, a mistake, a worry, whatever. Or we're at the office or in the shower, doing the very same thing—and it all seems so real.

When we are thinking, however, it's easy to lose sight of the fact that we think thoughts, not reality. Let me explain. It may seem strange, but most of us have a tendency to forget that we're thinking because it's something that we're always doing—like breathing. But until I mentioned breathing, you weren't really consciously aware that you were breathing—were you? Thinking works in a similar way. Because it's such a part of us, we tend to give enormous significance and take very seriously most of the thoughts that drift through our minds. We begin to treat our thoughts as if they were the real thing, allowing them to stress us out.

If you reflect on this idea, you'll probably be able to see the practical implications. When you have a thought, that's all it is—a thought. Thoughts certainly don't have the power or authority to stress you out without your conscious or unconscious consent. Thoughts are just images and ideas in your mind. They are like dreams—only you're awake while you're having them. But with waking thoughts, you get to decide how seriously you are going to take them.

For example, you might have a series of thoughts while driving to work: "Oh gosh, today is going to be really horrible. I've got six meetings and must finish those two reports by noon. I dread seeing Jane. I just know she's still going to be angry about the disagreement we had yesterday."

At this point, essentially only one of two things can happen. You will either take the thoughts seriously, start feeling worried, think about them some more, analyze how difficult your life has become, feel sorry for yourself, and so forth. Or if you recognize what has just happened, if you are consciously aware that you've just had a mini "thought attack," you can simply remind yourself that all that has occurred is yet another series of thoughts has traveled through your mind. You're not even at work yet—you're still driving in the car!

This doesn't mean that your day is going to be trouble-free or that you're pretending all is well and good. But think of how illogical it is to be having a bad day at work before your day officially begins. It's ludicrous—but that's precisely what most of us do all day long. We have thought after thought after thought. Yet we forget that it's thought. We treat it as real.

If you can change this way of relating to your thinking, you're going to be pleasantly surprised at how quickly and dramatically you will be able to reduce the stress in your work life. The next time you find yourself having a "thought attack," see if you can catch yourself. Then say something gentle to yourself like, "Whoops, there I go again," as a way of reminding yourself that you're taking your own thoughts a little too seriously. I hope you'll take this strategy to heart—it will make a world of difference.

57.

MAKE ALLOWANCES FOR

INCOMPETENCE

Like so many things, incompetence seems to be represented by a bell-shaped curve. There is always going to be a small percentage of people who are near the top, most people will fall somewhere near the middle, and a few will lie toward the bottom. In most professions (other than those where only highly competent people are considered qualified), it's just the way life seems to pan out. A few people in each field will be really good, most will be sort of average, and there will always be a few that make you wonder how in the world they manage to make a living.

It's interesting, however, that so many people don't seem to understand this dynamic or, if they do, they certainly don't exhibit any compassion or common sense in their reaction to it. Despite the fact that incompetence is an obvious and unavoidable fact of life, it's as though people are surprised, take it personally, feel imposed upon, and react harshly to it. Many people complain about incompetence, are bothered by it, discuss its rampant trend with others, and spend valuable time and energy hoping and wishing it would go away. I've seen people so upset about obvious incompetence that I thought they might have a heart attack or a nervous breakdown. Instead of seeing it as a necessary evil, they get all worked up, often compound the problem with their harsh reaction, and bang their head against the wall in frustration. In the end, nothing was accomplished except that the frustrated person had an emotional meltdown and made himself look bad.

One of my favorite television shows is the comedy "Mad About You." The brilliant comedian Lisa Kudrow plays the part of an almost unimaginably incompetent waitress in a cafe. I assumed her role was non-duplicable until recently when I was in a restaurant in Chicago. My waitress was so bad that, for a moment, I thought I was being "set up" with a hidden camera to see if I would sweat the small stuff. As far as I could tell, she managed to get every single order completely messed up. I ordered a vegetarian sandwich and ended up with rare roast beef. The customer next to me ordered a milk shake and ended up with a bottle of beer which was quickly spilled on his expensive looking shirt. It went on and on, each table seemingly worse than the next. After a while, it actually became amusing. When the check arrived, she had charged me for the roast beef, the other man's beer, and a T-shirt with the restaurant's logo!

Another story comes from someone I met who works in a real estate office. In addition to selling homes, she helps coordinate her clients with the various professionals who put the deal together—lenders, inspectors and appraisers. She told me of an appraiser she had worked with (twice) who had also worked with many of her colleagues. This appraiser was in her words, "beyond belief." His job was to appraise the market value of the home being sold to be sure the loan was a reasonable risk for the lender. Apparently, he was in the habit of appraising homes for up to twice their actual value. She was selling one home, for example, that was worth approximately $150,000 that he appraised for $300,000. The almost identical home next door sold for $150,000. She claimed that this was his standard operating procedure—he would toss out all rational and standard appraisal methods and rely on his "instinct." His incompetence must have worked out pretty well for the buyers—but imagine the risk the lenders were taking with home appraisals that had no relationship to reality.

The most unbelievable part of this story is that, allegedly, this appraiser has managed to stay in business for more than ten years! Despite a lengthy pattern of blatant incompetence, he continues to be hired by lenders who depend on his judgment to protect their loans.

In no way am I saying it's pleasant to deal with incompetence, but if you want to avoid feeling so irritated, it's important that you stop being so surprised and caught off guard by it. It's helpful to understand that some degree of incompetence is about as predictable as an occasional rainy day—even if you live in California, as I do. Sooner or later, it's bound to happen. So, instead of saying, "I can't believe my eyes," or something similar, keep in mind that it's bound to occur every once in a while—it's inevitable. This acceptance of the way things really are will probably allow you to say (or think) something like, "Of course it's going to be like this from time to time." You'll be able to keep your perspective and remember that, a vast majority of the time, it's not personally directed at you. Rather than focusing on the most dramatic and extreme examples to validate your belief in rampant incompetence, see if you can recognize and appreciate the fact that most people do really well, most of the time. With a little practice and patience, you'll cease being so upset over things you have very little control over.

I'm not suggesting that you should put up with or advocate incompetence, or that, if you're an employer, you shouldn't replace incompetent employees with harder-working, more qualified people. These are totally different issues. What I'm saying is that, regardless of who you are or what you do, you are going to run into (and have to deal with) at least some amount of incompetence in your work life. Why not learn to take it in stride, and not let it bother you so much?

By simply making allowances in your mind for something that is going to happen anyway, you'll be able to dramatically improve the quality of your life. I know that dealing with incompetence can be frustrating—especially when the stakes are high. I can virtually guarantee you, however, that losing your cool isn't going to help very much.

The next time you run into incompetence, even if it's flagrant, see if you can make the best of it, rectify the situation if possible, and then go on with your day. Let it go. Rather than turning the incompetence into front page news in your mind, see if you can turn it into just another minor story. If you do, you'll be free from yet another of life's sources of frustration.

58.

DON'T BE TOO QUICK
TO COMMENT

It's hard to quantify exactly how helpful this strategy has been in my own work life because often the results are subtle or speculative. I can say for sure, however, that it's been a significant and powerful tool. Learning to be less quick to comment has saved me from engaging in a great deal of unnecessary or untimely conversation. Without question, it's also saved me time, energy, and probably more than a few arguments.

Many of us are quick to comment on practically anything. We'll gladly comment on someone else's comment, their opinion, or a mistake that we perceive may have been made. We will offer our own opinion, comment on a policy, a pattern of behavior, or a personal gripe. Often we just want to get something off our chests. Sometimes when we're mad or frustrated, we'll blurt something out—an expression of the way we are feeling, or a defensive jab. We'll comment on the way someone looks, behaves, or seems to think. Sometimes our comments are critical in nature, other times they are complimentary or engaging. Often we'll share our vision, a belief, a potential solution, a prejudice, or a simple observation.

Obviously, there are times when other people ask that we comment or share our point of view. And a great deal of the time we are simply being responsive to the moment, and our comments are absolutely appropriate. In fact, this is probably the case a vast majority of the time. Most of our comments are probably useful, helpful, necessary, or simply entertaining. Sometimes our input can help solve a problem, come up with a solution, a better way of doing something, or contribute in some meaningful way. Terrific. Keep commenting.

Invariably, however, some of our comments are at best unnecessary and at worst counterproductive. They arise out of habit, a knee-jerk reaction, or some unexplained need we have to comment. Some of these comments lead to arguments, hurt feelings, or confusion. These are the ones that you want to avoid making, if possible.

Recently, a woman I met shared with me the following example. She had been working all day long and was just about to leave her office. She said she was dreaming of spending the evening alone—having a hot bath and curling up with a good book before bed. She saw a few coworkers down the hall and she walked over to say good night.

The others were discussing a heated issue that, in a practical sense, had little or no affect on her. No one even asked her opinion. Yet she had an idea she decided to share with the group. She said, "Do you know what you should do?" You can probably guess the rest of this story. Immediately, she was engaged in the conversation, and because she was the one who brought up the idea, it would have been inappropriate for her to leave. She spent the next hour and a half explaining and defending her position. In the end, there was no resolution. She went home exhausted, too tired to read. She had been looking forward to a peaceful evening. Instead, she ended up getting home late with a lot on her mind, feeling resentful and confused.

While the details are always a little different, there are hundreds, maybe even thousands of ways that most of us do something similar on a regular basis. This woman did nothing wrong; her only intention was to be helpful and friendly. Yet her simple, harmless comment led to a stressful free-for-all that wore her out. Are there times when it's appropriate to engage in this type of conversation? Of course there are. Yet her goal was to spend a quiet evening alone.

On many occasions, I've done essentially the same thing. For example, I'll be finishing a phone conversation and, at the very last second without thinking, I'll say "What ever happened to such and such?" My question will encourage the person I'm speaking with to launch into a detailed discussion and I'll be on the phone an extra twenty minutes. Meanwhile, someone else is waiting for me to return their call and now I'm running late. Isn't it obvious that, in instances such as these, I'm contributing to my own stress?

Occasionally, we'll blurt out a comment that has longer-term implications. I once heard a woman in a small office yell out to one of her coworkers, "You are the worst listener I've ever met. I hate talking to you." Had she been less quick to comment, she may have been able to reflect on a slightly less adversarial and more effective way to share her feelings.

The question is, how much stress could you avoid by simply learning to bite your tongue when it's in your best interest to do so? I've met more than a few people who claim that this simple change in habit has greatly contributed to a more peaceful life. They now say fewer things that they regret later by reflecting with wisdom before they speak. This is a fairly simple idea to implement into your life. For the most part, it involves nothing more than a gentle pause before you speak—just enough time to allow your wisdom to tell you whether what you are about to say is in your best interest. Give it a try. You may save yourself a great deal of grief.

59.

LET GO OF

"PERSONALITY CLASHES"

Invariably, as people share with me their list of gripes about their work, the subject of "personality clashes" is brought to my attention. People say things like, "I simply can't get along with certain types of people," and "Some personalities just don't match mine." The assumption is often made that certain personality types just don't mix—shy people can't get along with outgoing people, or sensitive individuals can't work well with more aggressive people, to name just a few. This is unfortunate because rarely can we pick and choose the types of personalities we work with. Instead, we usually get what we get. If we can't rise above the stereotypical assumptions regarding who can and can't work well together, we're out of luck, doomed to a life of frustration.

While it's easy to understand why some people make these assumptions, in reality there's no such thing as a personality clash. If there were, then our generalities would always apply—and they obviously do not. I've met tons of supposedly mismatched colleagues who are super team players and who love to work together. I'll bet you have too.

"I understand what you're saying, but my personality clashes are more specific and serious," I've been told by numerous employees. "For example, I can get along with some opinionated people, but not others. Sometimes two people just don't jell, and there is nothing you can do about it." While this can sometimes seem to be the case, to roll over and give in to the acrimonious feeling is self-defeating and, I believe, unnecessary.

Like everyone else, I prefer to work with certain types of people over others. For example, generally speaking, I'd prefer not to work with pushy people or those who are very hyperactive. I've found, however, that with some gentle effort on my part, along with some heightened perspective, I can usually work well with practically anyone, regardless of their personality type. The trick, I believe, lies in the word "gentle." It's critical to understand that our typical "roll up your sleeves and try hard" approach doesn't work very well when our goal is to overcome a difference in personality. In fact, the harder you try or the more you force the issue, the more it's going to seem that you're swimming upstream.

What works well for me is to think in terms of getting along as part of my job description. In other words, I attempt to take responsibility for making the relationship work; I put the ball in my own court. Rather than writing off the relationship (or my experience of the working relationship) as doomed for failure or frustration, I see if I can rise to the occasion and accept the challenge. Instead of seeing myself as good and the other person as flawed, I humorously label each of us as "characters," each playing a different role. I keep my spirit light and my sense of humor intact. Gently, I try to let go of my insistence that other people see life or behave the way I do. Almost without fail, this opens my heart and broadens my perspective.

Amy and Jan are fourth grade teachers at the same elementary school. I was told that the teachers were supposed to be working together to create a consistent curriculum for the students. The problem was, they couldn't stand each other and were constantly criticizing each other's teaching style. Apparently, both women felt they had an irreconcilable personality clash. In addition to a great deal of backstabbing and passive-aggressive jabs, the two of them engaged in a verbal confrontation in front of the parents at a parents and teachers meeting. Amy accused Jan of being "so undisciplined and detail-oriented that her students wouldn't be prepared for fifth grade level studies the following year." Jan barked back that Amy was "not only incompetent, but that parents should know that she played favorites and had tougher standards for the kids she didn't like."

Their inability to respect their differences and dismiss their childlike personality clash petrified the parents, who became visibly upset. The remainder of the school year was filled with stress, anger, and worry for the parents of the students, and self-created (and well-deserved) embarrassment for the two teachers. Instead of understanding that differences in personality and style can create a more interesting learning environment, the two of them took their differences personally and acted out their frustration. In this example, as in all others, no one wins.

Letting go of personality clashes in this way has made an enormous difference in my work life. I've been able to see that often it is to my advantage to work with people who are very different from me, and that ultimately it makes my work more interesting. I suggest you take a similar look at your own personality clashes. Letting them go will take a huge weight off your shoulders.

60.

DON'T GET STRESSED BY
THE PREDICTABLE

In many industries there are certain standard procedures or problems that are, to a large degree, predictable. The first few times they happen, or if you're caught off guard, it's understandable that they can create some anxiety or stress. However, once you factor them into your awareness, and you can predict how events are typically played out, it's silly to be annoyed and upset. Yet I find that many people continue to feel bothered and stressed, even after they see how the game is played. They continue to get upset, angry, and complain about a pattern that is predictable. To me, this is self-induced stress in its purest form.

I've had several fairly relaxed friends who are, or who have been, flight attendants for major airlines. Although they themselves are usually the type of people who take life in stride, they have shared with me some interesting stories about colleagues who fall apart (luckily without the passengers being aware) over absolutely predictable parts of their job.

One woman gets completely stressed out every time her flight is delayed. She calls her husband to complain about her stressful job, and shares her frustration with her friends (who have already heard the story hundreds of times). Rather than saying to herself, "Of course there are going to be occasional delays," she tortures herself by reacting to the predictable.

Another flight attendant (this one a male) gets super angry whenever he runs into a rude or unappreciative passenger. He's obviously bright enough to understand that this is bound to happen every once in a while (or probably more often than that). Yet, every time it happens, he goes crazy and feels compelled to share his anger with others. All he does is stir up the other flight attendants by getting them focused on the few disrespectful people instead of the vast majority who are quite pleasant.

I met an accountant who gets annoyed every March and April because his hours are increased and he can't leave the office at 5:00. He jumps up and down and complains about how "unfair" it is, even though it's absolutely predictable. It would seem to me that virtually *all* accountants who prepare income tax returns for a living would be the busiest during tax season. What am I missing?

I met a police officer who took it personally when people would drive faster than the speed limit. He would get frustrated and dish out harsh lectures, apparently forgetting that it was his job to catch people speeding to create safer roads. Again, this is a predictable part of his work. I've spoken to a number of other police officers who simply take this part of their job in stride—because they know it's coming, it's predictable. Most of them say, "Sure, we have to issue a citation, but why in the world would I get stressed out over it?"

Before you say, "Those are silly examples," or "I'd never get upset over something like that," take a careful look at your own industry. It's always easier to see why someone else shouldn't be upset than it is to admit that you, too, can make a bigger deal out of something than is really necessary. I admit I've made this mistake myself on more than one occasion, and perhaps you have too. By seeing certain aspects of your profession as predictable, you can alleviate a great deal of frustration.

Although the specific details and hassles are different in each industry and while many of the predictable events don't appear to make much sense, I've seen a similar pattern in many fields. In some industries, for example, there are built-in delays. You'll be waiting on suppliers, orders, or someone or something else in order to do your job, so it will always *seem* like you're running late and in an enormous hurry. And while it's true you have to wait until the last minute to get everything you need, it's entirely predictable and consistent—you know it's going to happen. Therefore, if you can make the necessary allowances in your mind for the inevitable, you won't have to feel the pressure. Instead, you learn to take it in stride. This doesn't mean you don't care. Obviously, it's necessary and appropriate to do your best job and work as quickly and efficiently as possible. To be surprised and resentful that you're constantly waiting for others is foolish.

In other fields (perhaps most of them), there is always more work to be done than time to do it. If you look around, you'll notice that everyone is in the same boat—it's set up that way. Work is designed to land on your desk slightly quicker than you're able to complete it. If you examine this tendency, you'll notice that it's absolutely predictable. If you worked twice as fast as you currently do, nothing would change in the sense of getting it all done. As you work faster and more efficiently, you'll notice that magically more work will appear. Again, this doesn't mean your work isn't demanding or that you shouldn't work hard and do your absolute best. It just means that you don't have to lose sleep over the fact that it's never going to be completely done—because it isn't.

As you see these and other work-related tendencies in their proper "predictable" perspective, you can eliminate a great deal of stress. You can make allowances in your mind, attitude, and behavior for that which you know is going to happen anyway. You can breathe easier and, perhaps, learn to relax a little more. I hope this added perspective is as helpful to you as it has been to me.

61.

STOP PROCRASTINATING

Recently I received a frantic phone call from an accountant that demonstrates one of the most widely used excuses for being late. She used the familiar statement, "It was really complicated and took a great deal of time." If you take a deep breath and a step back, I think you'll agree with me that, in a way, this is a ridiculous excuse that creates unnecessary grief for both the person being late, as well as the person who has to wait. All it really does is ensure that you'll continue to be late, as well as encourage you to feel victimized by a shortage of time.

Every project takes a certain amount of time. This is true whether it's a tax form, other paperwork, a report, the building of a house, or the writing of a book. And, although factors that are well beyond our control and completely unpredictable do come into play, the truth is, in a vast majority of cases, you can make a *reasonable* estimate of the amount of time you will need to complete the task even if you have to factor in some extra time for unknown elements.

For example, the accountant I'm referring to was well aware that there was some measure of complexity to her task and that she would have to factor the degree of difficulty into her time schedule. She also had the advantage, as the rest of us do, of knowing the exact date that Uncle Sam demands the complete return! Why then did she wait so long to begin? And why did she use the "really complicated" excuse instead of simply admitting that she waited too long to get started? It would have taken her exactly the same number of hours to complete the project, whether she had started a month earlier or had she waited even longer.

Many of us do the very same thing in our work as well as in our personal lives. I know plenty of people who are virtually *always* late, whether it's to pick up the kids in their car pool, sit down before church starts on Sunday, or prepare food for dinner guests. The interesting part of this tendency isn't the fact that they are always running late, but the excuses that are used: "I had to pick up three kids," "I had to make two stops before work," "It's tough to get everything done before I run out the door," "Having dinner guests is more work for me."

Again, I'm not denying that it is tough to get everything done—it is—but in all of these examples, you are working with absolutely known variables. You know exactly how many kids you have, how long it takes to get them ready and to get them where they need to be. You know how long it takes to drive to work, and that there will almost certainly be traffic to contend with. You are absolutely aware of the fact that having dinner guests can be a lot of work, and that it takes a certain amount of extra time to prepare dinner and get everything ready. When we use the "I didn't have enough time" excuse we are fooling ourselves, thus virtually guaranteeing that we will make the identical mistake next time.

To get over this tendency requires humility. The only solution is to admit that, in most instances, you do have the time, but you must start a little earlier and make whatever allowances are necessary to ensure that you won't be in a mad rush. So, if you're constantly running five minutes late, or thirty minutes late, and this is creating stress in your life and stress for other people, you need to make a real effort to start five minutes earlier, or thirty minutes earlier, on a consistent basis.

My deadline for completing this book was September 1 of last year. I had known that this was my deadline for over six months. I had been given plenty of time. Do you think it would have been a good idea for me to wait until July 15 to begin? Of course not. This would have created a great deal of unnecessary stress for myself and for my publisher. I would have been rushed, and wouldn't have been able to do my best job. Yet this is precisely what many people do in their work. They wait too long to begin, then complain about how much else they had going on.

Think of how much less stress would be in your life if you would simply begin your tasks a little earlier. Then rather than rushing from one project to the next, you'd have plenty of time. Rather than gripping the wheel and swerving your way from lane to lane to the airport or office, you'd arrive with a few minutes to spare. Rather than having the parents of the kids in your carpool angry and frustrated at you some, if not most of the time, you'd develop a reputation as a reliable and conscientious friend.

This is one of the simplest suggestions I've made in any of my books, yet in some ways it's one of the most important. Once you get in the habit of starting a little earlier, a great deal of your daily stress, at least that portion that you have some degree of control over, will fade away.

62.

CONFRONT GENTLY

It's hard to imagine working for a living without at least some degree of confrontation. After all, we live in a world of conflicting interests, desires, and preferences. We have different standards and expectations. A job that is considered well done and complete to one person may be woefully inadequate to another. Something that you consider to be an emergency or absolutely critical may seem almost irrelevant to someone else, or at least unworthy of their time. There are so many issues and people to deal with that an occasional confrontation seems inevitable. At times, you may have to confront someone in order to achieve a desired result, clarify an intention, shake someone up, make things happen, resolve a conflict, break out of a rut, or improve communication.

While confrontations may be inevitable, they don't necessarily have to seem like a war or lead to hurt or angry feelings, stress, or disappointment. Instead, it's possible to confront someone (or be confronted) in a gentle, effective way that leads not only to your desired result, but also in a way that brings the two of you closer together personally or professionally.

It seems to me that most people are too aggressive and defensive during confrontations. They lose their humanity and their humility. They approach the issue in a hostile way, as if they are right and the other person is wrong. It's "me against you," or "I'm going to teach you." The assumption seems to be that confrontations are by definition confrontational, and that being aggressive is the best approach.

If you're too aggressive, however, you're going to seem adversarial to others, thus encouraging them to become defensive. The people you confront will see you as difficult, as if you are the enemy. When people are defensive, they become poor listeners, incredibly stubborn, and seldom change their point of view or see their contribution to a problem. They don't feel respected and they lose their respect for you. So, if you are confronting someone in an aggressive way, chances are you're going to run into a brick wall.

The key to effective confrontation is to be firm yet gentle and respectful. Approach the confrontation with the assumption that there is a solution and that you will be able to work things out. Rather than assessing blame and assuming fault, try to see the innocence in yourself as well as in the other person. Rather than using phrases that are almost guaranteed to elicit a defensive response such as: "You've made a big mistake and we need to talk," try instead to say things with a little more humility, something like, "I'm a little confused about something—can you help me out?"

More important than the words you use, however, are your feelings. It's not always possible, but when it is, try to avoid confrontations when you're angry or stressed out. It's always best to wait a little while until you get your perspective, or until your mood rises. Keep in mind that most people are reasonable, respectful, and willing to listen when dealing with a calm, collected person who is speaking honestly from his heart.

When you approach your confrontations in a gentle manner, it not only produces more effective results, but it keeps your own stress level down as well. In other words, a gentle spirit is a relaxed spirit, even when it has to do something that is normally considered difficult. There is something very comforting about knowing that you're going to keep your cool regardless of what you must do. In addition, you'll have fewer battles to fight, and those that you do have will be shorter and less severe. You'll receive more cooperation and respect from others and, perhaps most importantly, your own thoughts and feelings will be much nicer.

The next time you confront someone, for whatever reason, I hope you'll consider doing it a little more gently. If you'd like for your life to seem less like a battle, this is an excellent place to start.

63

REMEMBER THE THREE R'S

If I asked you what I meant by the Three R's, many of you would probably guess, "Reading, writing, and arithmetic." I've developed my own three R's, however, that I feel are equally important, especially if you want to learn to be a less reactive, happier person. The three R's I'm referring to are: "Responsive, receptive, and reasonable."

"Responsive" means acting appropriately to the issue at hand. Rather than being driven and controlled by habitual, knee-jerk reactions, being responsive means having the ability to maintain perspective and to choose the best possible alternative or course of action, given your unique situation. Because they are able to see the entire picture so well, responsive individuals are able to factor into every equation all the variables, instead of being limited to their usual way of doing things. They are willing to change direction, if necessary, and admit their mistakes when appropriate.

For example, it's common for a builder to run into unexpected changes in the original plans—unknown soil conditions, a shortage of capital, or unforeseen design problems. A reactive builder will panic, overreact and become difficult to work with. A good builder will take the changes in stride, be responsive to the changes, rise to the occasion and get the job done.

"Receptive" implies being open to ideas and suggestions. It means you are inclined and willing to receive whatever it is that you need at that moment—data, creativity, a new idea, or whatever. It's the opposite of being closed-minded and stubborn. People who are receptive are willing to have a "beginner's mind," the willingness to learn, even if they are considered the expert. Because they are not defensive, these people have sharp learning curves and are almost always the ones who come up with the best ideas. They are fun to work with and are great team players because they think "outside the box" and consider differing points of view.

A retired CEO that I know is one of the most receptive individuals I've ever had the privilege of knowing. He was a business leader who was willing to listen to everyone—and who would frequently take the advice of his employees. Rather than stubbornly insisting that his answers were always the best, he would take his ego out of the picture and nondefensively reflect on the suggestions to determine the best possible course of action. He told me, "It made my job so much easier. By being genuinely receptive to suggestions and ideas, rather than shutting them off, I had the advantage of hundreds of brilliant minds working together—rather than having to rely on my tiny little mind."

"Reasonable" suggests the ability to see things fairly, without the self-serving justification that so often clouds our vision. It's the ability to see your own contribution to a problem and the willingness to listen to and learn from other points of view. Being reasonable includes the ability to put yourself in the shoes of others, being able to see the bigger picture, and to maintain perspective. People who are reasonable are well liked and highly respected. Because they are willing to listen, others pay close attention to what they have to say, as well. Reasonable people rarely have enemies, and their conflicts are kept to an absolute minimum. They are able to see beyond their own desires and needs, which makes them compassionate and helpful to others.

If you can strive to be responsive, receptive, and reasonable, my guess is that most everything else will fall into place and take care of itself.

64.

GET OUT OF THE
GRUMBLE MODE

Grumble, grumble, grumble. A great big sourpuss. Someone who takes himself, others, and everything else too seriously. The primary focus is on problems, always critical, frowning, angry, defensive, hurried, frustrated, and stressed. Someone who is waiting for life to get better, for things to be different. Is this you?

Now, use your imagination and zoom forward ten years, twenty, thirty. Are you still blessed with the gift of life? If not, you missed the point, and it's too late to do anything about it. While you're in the midst of your career, while there are problems to deal with, it seems as if life is going to last forever. Yet deep down we all know that in reality, life slips away too quickly. You had your chance to experience and explore life and its many facets—the beauty as well as the hassles. But in a way, you took it for granted. You spent your time grumbling, wishing life was different.

If, on the other hand, you are still lucky enough to be alive years down the road, looking back, are you happy that you were so serious and grouchy for all those years? If you could do it all again—if you could live your life over— are there things you'd do differently? Would you be a different person with a different attitude? Would you have more perspective?

If you knew right now what you're going to know then, would you take it all so seriously? Would you grumble so much?

We all get too serious at times. Perhaps it's human nature. Yet there's an enormous difference between someone who gets serious from time to time, and someone else who is constantly in the grumble mode. The good news is, it's never too late to change. In fact, once you see how ridiculous it is, you can change quickly.

A grumbler will blame life for his sour attitude. He will validate his negativity by pointing to the problems and hassles that he must face. He will justify his position by pointing out the injustices of life and the flaws of others. He hasn't a clue that his vision of life stems from his own thoughts and beliefs.

Charles Schulz has always been one of my favorite cartoonists. In one scene, Charlie Brown's head is hanging and he's slouching his shoulders. While frowning, he explains to Linus that if you want to be depressed, it's important to stand in this posture. He goes on to explain that if he were to stand up straight, lift his head and shoulders, and smile, he wouldn't be able to remain depressed.

In the same way, a grouch can begin to feel better by recognizing the absurdity of a negative attitude. Ideally, to cure yourself of this, you'll want to experience a major insight—a feeling of "I can't believe I was really that way." In order to shift from grumble mode to a less serious nature, you'll need to get a sense of humor—the ability to look back at the way you used to be, and chuckle.

The world has become too serious. If you're part of this sad trend, it's time to change. Life is really short. It's too important to take so seriously.

65.

GET IT OVER WITH

Sometimes it's helpful to be reminded of the obvious—especially when it involves something that is frightening, unpleasant, or uncomfortable. As you undoubtedly already know, it's easy to look at your list of things to do and avoid, procrastinate, postpone, or even conveniently forget that which you least want to do. Somehow you find a way to save the worst for last.

I've created a habit for myself that has undoubtedly saved me thousands of hours of unnecessary stressful or worrisome thinking. The habit I'm referring to involves attending to the most difficult or uncomfortable parts of my day first, before anything else; getting them out of the way.

For example, I may have to resolve a conflict, make a difficult phone call, deal with a sensitive issue, engage in a confrontation, turn someone down or disappoint them, or something else that I wish I didn't have to do. I've made a commitment to myself that, whenever possible and practical, I make that phone call first—before anything else. I get it over with! That way, I avoid all the stress that would have been inevitable had I waited. But even more than that, I find that I'm usually more effective in dealing with the situation because I'm fresher and more alert. I haven't spent the day dreading or rehearsing my conversation. This makes me more responsive to the moment, a key element in solving most problems effectively and gracefully.

Without question, saving the most uncomfortable parts of your day for last is an extremely stressful thing to do. After all, it's not going to go away—so it's hanging over your head. Even if you're not consciously thinking or worrying about whatever it is you have to do (which you probably are), you're still aware of it. It's looming. The longer you wait, the more likely you are to blow it out of proportion, imagine the worst, and get yourself all worked up. While all this mental activity is going on, you remain tense and stressed, which of course, causes you to sweat practically everything that comes your way. On a more subtle level, this fear and anxiety that you are feeling is a distraction to your concentration. This affects your performance, judgment, and perspective.

The simple solution is to dive in and get it over with, whatever "it" happens to be. You'll breathe a sigh of relief when it's over and done with. You can then get on with the rest of your day.

I'm sure there are exceptions, but I've yet to experience a single scenario where I've regretted this decision. I know for sure that this strategy has helped me to keep calmer and, overall, happier while I'm engaged in my work. My only concern in sharing this strategy with you is now whenever I call someone first thing in the morning (assuming they have read this book), they might assume we have an issue to resolve.

66.

DON'T LIVE IN AN
IMAGINED FUTURE

If you want to be a happier, less-stressed person, there is no better place to start than with becoming aware of what I like to call "anticipatory thinking," or an imagined future. Essentially, this type of thinking involves imagining how much better your life will be when certain conditions are met—or how awful, stressful, or difficult something is going to be at some point down the road. Typical anticipatory thinking sounds something like this: "I can't wait to get that promotion, then I'll feel important." "My life will be so much better when my 401K is fully funded." "Life will be so much simpler when I can afford an assistant." "This job is only a stepping stone to a better life." "These next few years will be really tough, but after that I'll be cruising." You get so carried away by your own thoughts that you remove yourself from the actual present moments of your life, thereby postponing the act of living effectively and joyfully.

There are other, more short-term forms of this type of thinking as well: "The next few days are going to be unbearable," "Boy, am I going to be tired tomorrow," "I just know my meeting is going to be a disaster," "I know my boss and I are going to argue again the next time we meet," "I'm dreading training that new employee." There are endless variations of this stressful tendency. The details are usually different, but the result is the same—stress!

"I used to worry so much about my upcoming annual reviews," said Janet, a comptroller at an auto parts manufacturer. "Finally I decided I had to break my habit. My worry was eating me up and draining my energy. I realized that only once in fifteen years had I been given a negative review—and even then, nothing bad happened. What's the point of worry anyway? What we worry about rarely happens, and even when it does, the worry doesn't help."

Gary, a restaurant manager, described himself as a "world-class worrywart." Every night, he anticipated the worst—hostile or dissatisfied customers, stolen food, contaminated meat, an empty room—"You name it, I worried about it." At the time, he considered himself somewhat wise, as if his anticipatory thinking would head off certain negative events. After many years of anticipating the worst, however, he concluded that, in reality, the opposite was true. He began to see that his worrisome thinking would, in some cases, create problems that weren't really there. To quote Gary, "I would work myself up into a lather and get really upset. Then, because I was anticipating the worst and expecting everyone to make mistakes, I'd be unforgiving of really minor things—a waitress would mix up an order and I'd chew her out. She would become so upset and worried that she'd start making much more serious mistakes. Looking back, most of it was my own fault."

Obviously, some planning, anticipating, and looking forward to future events and accomplishments are an important and necessary part of success. You need to know where you'd like to go in order to get there. However, most of us take this planning far too seriously and engage in futuristic thinking far too often. We sacrifice the actual moments of life in exchange for moments that exist only in our imaginations. An imagined future may or may not ever come true.

Sometimes people ask me, "Isn't it exhausting and unbearable being on a promotional tour—a new city every single day, living out of a suitcase for weeks at a time?" I admit that occasionally I do get really tired, and sometimes I even complain about it, but in reality it's a lot of fun as long as I take it one event at a time. If I spend a great deal of time and energy, however, thinking about how many interviews I have tomorrow, my next ten public appearances, or tonight's long airplane flight, it's predictable that I'll be exhausted and overwhelmed. Whenever we focus too much on all there is to do instead of simply doing what we can in this moment, we will feel the stress associated with such thinking.

The solution for all of us is identical. Whether you're dreading tomorrow's meeting, or next week's deadline, the trick is to observe your own thoughts caught up in the negative expectations and imagined horrors of the future. Once you make the connection between your own thoughts and your stressful feelings, you'll be able to step back and recognize that if you can rein in your thoughts, bringing them back to what you are actually doing—right now—you'll have far more control over your stress level.

67.

MAKE SOMEONE ELSE
FEEL GOOD

After years of working in the stress reduction field, teaching people to be happier, I'm still amazed that some of the most effective methods of reducing one's stress and of improving one's life are actually the simplest. One of the first real-life lessons my parents taught me when I was a child is perhaps the most basic of all: If you want to feel good about yourself, make someone else feel good! It really is that simple. Perhaps it is because this idea is so simple that we sometimes forget to do it.

I've attempted to implement this bit of wisdom into my work life for as long as I can remember. I'd say that the results are nearly perfect. It seems that anytime I go out of my way to make someone else feel good, it ends up brightening my day and making myself feel better as well. It reminds me that so often the nicest things in life aren't "things." Instead, they are the feelings that accompany acts of kindness and nice gestures. It's clear to me that "what goes around, does indeed come around."

Whether it's remembering a birthday with a thoughtful card, taking the time to write a note of congratulations for a job well done, a written or verbal compliment, a friendly phone call, an unasked-for favor, a bouquet of flowers, a note of encouragement, or any number of other possibilities, making someone else feel good—however you do it—is almost always a good idea.

Acts of kindness and good will are inherently wonderful. There's an old saying: "Giving is its own reward." This is certainly true. Your reward for being kind and making someone else feel good are the warm, positive feelings that invariably accompany your efforts. So, starting today, think of someone you'd like to make feel better and enjoy your rewards.

68.

COMPETE FROM THE HEART

Competition is a fact of life. To pretend that it doesn't exist or that you should avoid it all costs would be ridiculous. I've always loved to compete. As a child I was the fastest runner at school and the number one tennis player in Northern California in my age group. I was a high school All-American Athlete and went on to receive a college scholarship in tennis, where I played in the number one position and became the youngest captain in my team's history. I've run three marathons, one of them in three hours.

As an adult, my love of competition has continued, not only in sports, but in business as well. I love to negotiate, buy low, and sell high. I'm proud to be creative, and I'd like to believe I have a flair for marketing. The publishing world is fiercely competitive. I love to see my books doing well, and it's fun to get a standing ovation after a speech. I could certainly make the argument that if I didn't compete well, I wouldn't be helping very many people. So it's important that I compete.

I tell you these things because I've spoken to many people who assume that I'm too relaxed to compete, which is not true. I don't want to give the impression, as I suggest you compete from the heart, that you can't compete effectively if you are a gentle person and become less attached to winning. You can have it all. You can be a winner and financially successful, have fun, compete hard, but never lose your perspective of what's most important—enjoying yourself, giving back, and taking it all in stride.

To compete from the heart means that you compete less from a desperate or neurotic need to achieve and more out of a love for what you do. Competing is its own reward. You are completely immersed in the process, absorbed in the present moments of the activity—the business deal, the sale, the negotiation, interaction, or whatever. When you compete from your heart, the process itself provides the satisfaction; winning is secondary. When looked at in this healthier way, your business life becomes so much easier. You play hard—and then let go. You bounce back almost instantly. You're resilient. You're a good sport. By not being so attached to a specific outcome (winning), you conserve energy and see hidden opportunities. You learn from your mistakes and losses. You move forward. Isn't it obvious that this not-so-attached attitude is in your best interest?

It's been said, "Winning isn't everything, it's the only thing." To me, this is utter nonsense. This philosophy stems from the fear that if you aren't consumed with winning, you never will win. I can tell you that I'm not consumed with winning—never have been, never will be—yet I've won many awards, contests, and first-place finishes. I've also done well financially and made some wise investments. But none of my competitive accomplishments would mean anything to me if they weren't from the heart—if I became so carried away with the competition and outcome that I forgot my humanity. So, to me, the "Winning is everything" motto is grossly inaccurate.

"Maybe it's just because I'm older now, but ever since I turned fifty,

I've become much softer," says Mary, a television producer. "Looking back, I realize how incredibly harsh I was, and how unnecessarily mean-spirited I could be. I'd reject people and their ideas as if they were disposable diapers. People must have hated me. It's weird—but now, I'm just as discriminating and picky as before, but when I have to reject someone, I do so with compassion, without making them feel worse than they already do. I like myself better now, too."

Ed worked for a bio-technology company for five years. Part of his job was to consolidate, cut costs and help his company become "lean." He told me something so awful I almost didn't believe him. "I hate to admit it, but I used to get a thrill out of firing people. I didn't think of myself as a horrible person or anything like that, but cutting costs meant more to me than the effects it had on the people involved. That's how I measured my effectiveness, and that's how I was judged. The fact that these people were scared and didn't know what to do, or that they had three children to support and rent to pay, had no effect on me whatsoever. Then, one day it happened to me! Out of the blue, I was fired, or 'let go' as they put it. I'm sure many people were happy and thought I deserved it. I suppose I did, but I can tell you that, painful as it was, it was probably the best thing that ever happened to me—it opened my eyes to my compassion. I'll never treat people like that again."

Beyond the inaccuracy of this fearful attitude are the social implications. Competing only to win creates poor losers and poor winners. Psychological message: Unless you win, you must feel terrible. This sends a harmful message to kids and feeds into a sense of self-importance that is not only unhealthy, but ugly. How about this message instead:

Give it your very best effort, compete hard, enjoy every moment—and, if you should lose, be happy anyway. This is competing from the heart.

To compete from the heart is a gift, not only to yourself but to those to whom you are a role model and to the world at large. When you compete in this healthier, more loving way, you get the best of both worlds—achievement and perspective.

69.

BACK OFF WHEN YOU
DON'T KNOW WHAT TO DO

Without question, this is one of the most important mental techniques I have ever learned. In fact, it's become more of a way of life than a simple technique. It's made me more productive and, what's more, it's definitely helped me to sweat the small stuff less often at work.

It's tempting, when you don't know what to do, when you don't have an immediate answer, to try to force the issue. You try harder, think faster, attempt to figure things out, and struggle to come up with something. You give it your best shot.

At least that's what most of us assume. The problem is, it usually isn't your "best shot."

It seems ironic, yet often the most powerful and productive thing to do when you don't have an immediate answer to a problem is to gently back off of your thinking, consciously ease up, let go, and extend less effort. Doing so frees your mind and allows your innate intelligence and wisdom to come into play. Put another way, when you feel pressured and stressed, your wisdom is obstructed. But, as you ease off your thinking, it's free to surface and help you. Ideas will come to you.

Most of us have had the experience of (metaphorically) banging our head against a wall, struggling to make a decision or solve a problem. It's so complicated and difficult you simply don't know what to do. There doesn't appear to be any good solution. You're so frustrated that essentially you give up. A few minutes (or hours) later, you're doing something unrelated to your concern. You're thinking about something else when, out of the blue, an answer pops into your head. But not just any answer—a really good one. "That's it!" you rejoice.

This process isn't a matter of good luck. The truth is, our minds are more creative, solution-oriented, clever, and receptive to new answers when we aren't trying so hard—when we relax. This is difficult to accept because it seems important to work hard. And, of course, it is important to work hard. It's just that it's not always to your advantage to think so hard. We mistakenly believe that when we relax, our minds stop working. This is far from true. When we quiet the mind, it's still working—only in a different way.

When your mind is active, full speed ahead, it tends to spin and churn. An over-active mind often goes over the same set of facts again and again, encouraging you to think "inside the box." Your thinking becomes repetitive and habitual because it's going over that which it already knows or believes to be true. Because you're working so hard, you use a great deal of energy, creating unnecessary stress and anxiety. You can probably guess that an overactive mind is the perfect environment for sweating the small stuff.

Somewhere in all the churning of an overactive mind, your wisdom and common sense are lost. These invisible, usually overlooked qualities get buried in a sea of activity and you fail to see the obvious. I know it seems strange that less effort is better, but it's really true. I hope you'll give this strategy a try because I'm virtually certain that it can help your work life become a great deal easier.

70.

ADMIT THAT IT'S YOUR CHOICE

This can be a difficult strategy to embrace. So many people resist it, yet if you can embrace it, your life can begin to change—immediately. You will begin to feel more empowered, less victimized, and as if you have more control of your life. Not a bad set of rewards for a simple admission of the truth.

The admission I'm referring to is your choice of career and the accompanying hassles. You must admit that, despite the problems, limitations, obstacles, long hours, difficult coworkers, political aspects, sacrifices you make, and all the rest, that you are doing what you are doing because you have made the choice to do so.

"Wait a minute," I've been told so many times, "I'm doing what I'm doing, not by choice, but because I have to. I have no choice." I know it can seem that way. Yet if you think through this issue in a reflective way, you'll begin to see that in reality it really is your choice.

When I suggest that you admit that your job or career is your choice, I'm not saying that your problems are necessarily your fault, or that it's realistic that you make other choices. What I am suggesting is that ultimately, all things considered (including necessity, lifestyle choices, income needs, and the possibility of losing your job or even your home), you've made the decision to do what you're doing. You have weighed the options, considered your alternatives, studied the consequences, and, after all is said and done, you've decided that your best alternative is to do exactly what you are doing.

Chris, who works for a large advertising firm, resented this suggestion. In a bitter tone of voice, he told me, "That's absolutely ridiculous. I'm not choosing to work twelve hours a day on these stupid campaigns; I'm forced to. If I didn't work so hard, I'd be blackballed as lazy and go nowhere in this business or in the entire industry."

Can you see what a corner this man had painted himself into? Despite being a bright, up-and-coming advertising account executive, he felt trapped and resentful, a victim of "the way things have to be." He felt absolutely out of the loop when it came to taking any responsibility for his career choices and how hard he was working. The problem is, when you feel trapped and as if you aren't making your own choices, you feel like a victim.

Despite his objections, Chris had decided that it was worth it to work twelve hours a day. His decision was that, all things considered, he'd rather stay in his current position than go through the hassles, risk, and fear of looking for another job, making less money, losing his prestige, missing out on his chance to advance his career, and so forth. I can't tell you if his decision was a good one or not, but isn't it obvious that this was his choice?

Megan, a single mother, had a full-time job as a nurse, but dreamed of becoming a hospital administrator. When I met her at a book signing, she confessed to having spent the previous eight years convincing herself that she was a victim. Frequently, she would tell others, "I'd love to pursue my dream but it's impossible—look at my life."

Despite the very real difficulties she was facing, her greatest obstacle was her unwillingness to admit that her profession was her choice, as was her decision to stay right where she was. She had access to a good school, the grades to be admitted, and some good friends who would help her out with her daughter. None of that mattered, however, because she was a single mom.

The way she described her transformation, one of her friends had convinced her to stop blaming her circumstances. Somehow, she listened, and had the humility to make the change.

The way she put it, "The moment I admitted that *I* was the choice-maker, everything fell into place. I was able to enroll in the part-time night school program, and I'm already a third of the way through. It's frightening to think about how much I was getting in my own way. I realized that I may be a single mom for the rest of my life."

From time to time, most of us fall into the trap of believing that our circumstances are entirely beyond our control. Taking responsibility for your choices, however, takes you out of any "poor me" thinking and into an empowering, "I'm in charge of my own life" mind-set. I hope you'll reflect on this strategy because I'm confident that if you do, you'll feel less stressed and significantly more successful.

71.

BEFORE BECOMING DEFENSIVE,
TAKE NOTE OF WHAT
IS BEING SAID

This is a stress-reducing trick I learned many years ago. Essentially, all that this strategy involves is making the decision to step back, breathe, relax, and genuinely listen before you react or feel defensive. That's it. This simple commitment will help keep you from becoming defensive.

Reacting in a defensive manner usually involves a knee-jerk or instantaneous reaction to something that is being said. Someone makes a comment and you feel hurt. Someone deals you some constructive criticism and you feel the need to defend yourself, your work, your honor, or your point of view. Then after reacting defensively, you continue to think about what was said or what was done. You may even reply with some form of criticism of your own, or get into some kind of power struggle or argument, which usually only serves to escalate the situation.

Suppose your boss takes a quick look at something you've spent months working on. You've poured your best efforts and many late nights into the project. You're proud of your work and expect that others will be too. Your boss, however, says something less than kind. She obviously doesn't appreciate what went into your efforts, nor is she impressed. Her comment is something to the effect of "Couldn't you have done this differently?"

Most people are annoyed if not angered or hurt by this type of insensitive comment. And in case you've not noticed, many people therefore feel hurt and defensive a great deal of the time. It would be nice if everyone were kind regarding their reactions to us and our work, but unfortunately, that's not the world we live in.

If you implement this strategy into your reactions, you would in effect create a buffer or space between the comment and your defensive reaction—time for you to gather your composure and perspective. Does the comment make sense? Is there an element of truth in it? Can you learn something here? Or is the person simply being a jerk? The more honestly you can assess the situation, the more helpful it will be.

While it's not always easy, it sure pays huge dividends to take careful note of what is being said—before becoming defensive. If you do, you'll find yourself becoming less defensive on a regular basis.

72.

COMPLETE AS MANY
TASKS AS POSSIBLE

I don't think most people realize how stressful it can be to have multiple incomplete tasks hanging over your head. Just in case you are one of these people, let me assure you, it is stressful. I like to call this the "almost finished syndrome." It has always intrigued me because often, it would be relatively easy to simply bear down and complete something—not almost complete something, but really complete it 100 percent, and get it out of the way.

On many occasions, I've hired people for everything from a building or repair project around the house to an editing job at work. The person I've hired has been competent, creative, hard-working, skilled and motivated. Yet for some strange reason, they won't quite finish the job. Sure, they almost finish—sometimes they are about 99 percent done, but that last remaining bit seems to hang over their heads (and mine too). Often the last 1 percent takes as long as the first 99 percent.

When you absolutely finish a project, several good things happen. First, you enjoy the nice feeling of a sense of completion. It feels good knowing you've set out to do something and it's done, it's out of the way. Completion allows you to move forward without the distraction of having things hanging over your head.

Beyond the obvious, however, is the respect you feel for yourself and the respect you secure from others when you complete something. You said you were going to do something, and you did it—all of it. You send the message to others that "I am a person of my word," "You can trust me," and "I am reliable." And you affirm the message to yourself: "I am competent and trustworthy." This makes people want to help you—and want to refer business to you and want you to succeed.

Whether you are working for a corporation or a customer, it's undeniable that people will be irritated at you if you don't complete your tasks as agreed. Further, they will be on your back, complaining to you and about you. How can this be worth the stress it so obviously creates? Wouldn't it be easier to simply plan ahead and do whatever is necessary to get the job done—all the way done?

This is an easy habit to break. Take an honest look at your own tendencies. If you are someone who often almost finishes something, take note of the tendency and commit yourself to that last final completion. You can do it—and when you do, your life is going to seem so much easier.

73.

SPEND TEN MINUTES A DAY
DOING ABSOLUTELY NOTHING

I'll bet you're already thinking, "I could never do that," "He doesn't understand how busy I am," or "What a waste of time." If so, I'm happy to tell you that you're off base on all counts. The truth is, I absolutely understand how busy you must be, and I'm certain beyond any doubt that ten minutes of doing absolutely nothing can be the most productive ten minutes of your entire day.

It's precisely because you're so busy that spending ten minutes a day doing nothing is such a great idea. For most of us, a typical workday is sort of like a horse race—the moment we're out of bed, the race has begun. We start out fast and increase our speed as the day goes on. We rush around doing things, being productive, solving problems, and checking items off our ever-so-important "to do" list. It's really no wonder we're sweating the small stuff. Collectively, we're so busy that when the slightest glitch occurs or when something goes wrong, we fall apart and feel frustrated.

Spending a few minutes doing nothing, sitting still, embracing the silence helps prevent you from falling apart. It gives you a chance to regain your perspective and to access a quiet part of your brain where your wisdom and common sense exist. When you sit still and do nothing, it allows your mind the opportunity to sort things out and settle down. It turns what usually looks like chaos into a more manageable moment and provides your mind with a chance to rest and regroup. Ideas and solutions will pop into your head that would never have done so in a frenetic state of mind. When you're finished doing nothing or sitting still, it will often seem like life is coming at you a little slower, which makes everything seem a whole lot easier and less stressful.

One of the most successful CEOs that I've ever met does just this. Every day, regardless of how busy he is, he picks a time to enjoy his few minutes of quiet. He realizes that the busier he is, the more it's needed. He jokingly told me, "My quiet time has made me realize how much idle chatter runs through my mind, mostly nonsense. Clearly, all that noise gets in the way of my being able to see right to the heart of the matter. A few minutes of doing nothing usually cuts through the clutter."

Clearly, there are times when we are trying too hard or moving too fast. This is the ideal time to put on the brakes and quiet down. At first glance, this concept may seem counterproductive. Yet one of the most powerful and sure ways to achieve even more success in your life is to do absolutely nothing for a few minutes a day. You won't believe what you discover.

74.

LEARN TO DELEGATE

For obvious reasons, learning to be a better delegator can make your life easier. When you allow others to help you, when you put your faith in them and trust them, it frees you up to do what you do best.

I've found, however, that many people—even very high-achieving, talented and successful people—are often very poor delegators. The feeling is, "I might as well do it myself—I can do it better than anyone else." There are several major problems with this attitude. First of all, no one can do all things or be two places at once. Sooner or later, the magnitude of responsibility will catch up with you. Because you're so scattered, you'll be doing a lot of things, but the quality of your work will suffer. Learning to delegate helps to solve this problem by keeping you focused on what you're most qualified to do and that which you enjoy doing. In addition, when you don't delegate properly, you aren't allowing others the privilege of showing you what they can do. So, in a way, it's a little selfish.

Jennifer is a mortgage broker in a busy downtown office. Ironically, one of her biggest problems may have been that she was talented and highly competent at practically everything! She felt so secure about her ability to accomplish tasks, that she had become frightened at delegating almost any authority or responsibility. Whether it was making phone calls, negotiating with lenders, communicating with clients, or filling out paperwork, she was involved and on top of it all.

For a while, she managed to juggle things pretty well. As the years went by, however, and her time became more in demand, her unwillingness to delegate responsibility began to catch up with her. She was making more mistakes and becoming increasingly frustrated, forgetful, and stressed out. The people she worked with claimed she had become more short-tempered and arrogant.

At a seminar designed to help her prioritize more effectively, it became obvious to her that her greatest professional weakness was her unwillingness to delegate and share responsibility. She learned the obvious—-that no one can do everything indefinitely, and keep doing it well.

As she began to delegate responsibility—little things as well as those more important—she began to see light at the end of the tunnel. Her mind calmed down, and she began to relax. She could see more clearly where her talent could be used and where her time was best spent. She told me, "I'm back to my old self again."

Often it not only helps you but someone else when you delegate at work. When you ask for help, share responsibility, or delegate authority, you are often giving someone a chance to show you, or someone else, what they can do. In the publishing world, a senior editor might allow an associate editor to do some editing on a particular book, even though it's one of her favorite authors. This not only frees the senior editor's time, it also gives the associate editor a chance to show what she can do—so that she can enhance her career. My friends in the legal and corporate worlds say it works in the same way. Partners in law firms delegate a great deal of work to younger lawyers. Managers of corporations do the same to their less-experienced coworkers. I know that a cynic will say, "The only reason people delegate is to shove off the tough and dirty work on others." And, yes, there are plenty of people who look at it that way—but you don't have to. The point is, there are good reasons—in addition to selfish ones—to practice delegation.

I've seen flight attendants who are masters at delegation. Somehow they are able to get everyone working as a team, so that everyone's job is a bit easier. I've seen others who insist on doing everything themselves. They are the ones who seem the most stressed, and who make the passengers wait the longest. I've seen great chefs delegate certain chores—chopping, for instance—not because they don't like to do it, but because it allows them to focus on other aspects of food preparation that they excel at.

Whether you work in a restaurant, office, airport, retail outlet, or practically anywhere else, learning to delegate can and will make your life a bit easier. Obviously, there are select professions and positions that don't lend themselves well to delegation. For a good number of people, there's no way to say, "Here, you do it." If you fall into this category, perhaps you can practice at home. Can your spouse or roommate help you? Can you delegate certain chores to your kids? Might it be a good idea to hire someone to clean your home, change your oil, or something else that is time-consuming? If you think about your specific circumstances, you'll probably be able to think of at least a few ways to become a better delegator. If you do, you'll free up some time and make your life easier.

75.

STRENGTHEN YOUR PRESENCE

Whether you sell hot dogs to the public or work for IBM, strengthening your presence will make your experience of work more effective and enjoyable. It will enhance your rapport and connection with others, sharpen your concentration, and dissolve your stress.

Presence is a magical quality that is difficult to define. In fact, it's easier to describe its absence. In other words, you can usually tell in an instant the difference between someone who has it—and someone who doesn't. A person with powerful presence is said to be charismatic and magnanimous—people are drawn to his or her energy.

Having a strong presence does not necessarily mean you are outgoing, although it might. It's more a matter of being centered in yourself, comfortable with who you are, and completely absorbed in the moment. When you have a strong presence, the people you are with sense that you are truly "right there" with them, fully present. Your mind isn't drifting somewhere else. Instead, you are focused on what's going on and you are truly listening to what is being said. All of your energy is focused on the person who is talking to you.

So much of the stress that we experience has to do with our minds being in too many places at the same time. We are doing one thing, yet preoccupied with a dozen others. We're distracted by our own thoughts, concerns, and worries. Being present eases our stress because our minds are drawn back to this particular moment, fully attentive to the task at hand. We begin to operate at an optimal mental pace with near-perfect concentration. Although we are working smarter and more effectively, we become calmer and more relaxed.

Our stress is further reduced because of the increased enjoyment we experience. It's difficult to experience genuine satisfaction when your mind is too busy, scattered here and there, thinking about three or four things at once. Yet when your mind is focused, when you are fully present and engaged, your world comes alive. Everyday, ordinary experiences are seen in a new light. In many instances, they begin to appear quite extraordinary. Think about your hobbies. There's nothing inherently exhilarating about bird watching, knitting, or tinkering with your car. However, when you are fully present, these activities and so many others come alive—they become genuine sources of satisfaction. When you are fully present, something as simple as reading a book can become, for the moment, the most intriguing part of your life. You become lost in the story. Yet when you lack focus, that same book can seem boring and insignificant.

When you have presence with others, they are drawn to you. They relax around you and become undefensive. They enjoy your company and feel your sincerity; they feel important when they are with you. They want to do business with you and see you succeed. They are highly cooperative and rarely adversarial. They respect your boundaries and your wishes, and listen to what you have to say. Presence makes every interaction you have more interesting, since every conversation is a potential source of joy. In the absence of presence, all of this disappears. Interactions become habitual, lifeless, and boring.

Sometimes you meet someone and think to yourself, "There is something special about that person. I can't quite put my finger on it, but something is there." So often that "something" is presence.

The way to strengthen your presence is to understand its value. Make an ongoing effort to stop your mind from wandering. When you are with someone, be *with* them. When your mind wanders, gently bring it back. When you are doing something, don't be thinking about something else. Try to have more presence, see it as a worthwhile goal, and it will appear in your life. Once you experience its value—and feel the effects—there will be no turning back. You'll be hooked.

76.

LEARN TO SAY NO
WITHOUT GUILT

One of the ways that many of us get ourselves into trouble is that we commit to too many things; we fail to say no. We say, "Sure, I'll do it," or "No problem, I'll take care of it," when deep down, we know we don't really want to, or that we already have too much on our plates.

The problem with always saying yes is two-fold. First, the end result is almost always feeling overwhelmed, stressed and tired. There is simply a point when enough is enough, a point of diminishing return when our attitude, spirit, even our productivity begins to suffer. Our work suffers, as does our personal and family life. By saying yes too often, we begin to feel victimized and resentful that we have so much to do. Because we tend to feel guilty when we say no, it's often difficult to see that *we* were the ones who got ourselves into this mess by failing to say no more often.

The second major problem with failing to say no when it's appropriate to do so is that you end up with a slightly disingenuous attitude. In other words, you are doing things you really don't want to be doing or shouldn't be doing—but you are acting, on the surface, as if everything is just fine. For example, you'll agree to perform a task or switch shifts with a coworker by saying, "Oh, it's all right," when what you really need is a day off to yourself. Then because you don't get your much-needed rest, you feel victimized by your overwhelming schedule or angry that so many people ask favors of you! Again, you played a key role in the creation of your own stress, but you believe the stress is caused by outside forces, or that it's inevitable.

Saying no without guilt is not selfish—it's a protective necessity. If someone said to you, "Can I have the air you breathe?" you'd probably question their sanity. You certainly wouldn't feel guilty saying no. Yet if someone says, "Can I ask you to do something for me that will push you over the edge and make you feel stressed out and resentful?", there are many times that you'll agree either out of habit, obligation, or simply guilt. Sure, the person probably didn't phrase the request like that, but in reality, that's what is being asked of you.

Obviously there are many times that we can't say no, and many other times when it's in our best interest to say yes or that we simply want to say yes. Terrific! The trick is to use our wisdom, instead of old knee-jerk reactions, to decide when to say yes and when to say no. The key is to be reflective and to ask yourself, "All things considered—e.g., the feelings and needs of the person making the request, the need to say yes, and most importantly my own sanity, is it in my best interest to say yes, or is it okay to refuse? I think you'll discover that, put in this perspective, there are probably many instances when it's perfectly fine to say no.

77.

TAKE YOUR NEXT
VACATION AT HOME

This is a strategy I began using a number of years ago. To be honest, the first few times I gave it a try, I felt sure I was going to be giving up something—fun, relaxation, "my big chance to get away"—and that I would end up disappointed. However, I can honestly say that every time I have stayed home for my vacation, I'm really glad I did. Never once have I regretted my decision.

Vacations are something most people look forward to. They are usually wonderful, well-deserved, and almost always needed. However, a vacation which is ideally designed to be relaxing, rejuvenating, and energizing can at times bring on more stress than it eliminates. Here's a scenario. You finally get a week off. You have a great trip planned, yet you still have to do all that's necessary to leave. You rush to pack and to get all the loose ends and assorted details attended to. You're exhausted. It feels like you haven't had a chance to sit still for weeks. Yet here you are, running to catch another airplane, or rushing out the door to avoid traffic. In a way it seems like you're *speeding up so that you can slow down.* You want to get the most out of your vacation, so you won't be back until late next Sunday night—so you can start work again early the next day. Even before you leave, you know it's going to be tough coming back.

Part of you can't wait to leave because you know you're going to have a great time and get away from your normal routine—but the other part would love the chance to piddle around the house, curl up with a great book, start that yoga or exercise program, or maybe take a couple of simple, but relaxing day trips closer to home. But all that will have to wait because you're going on vacation.

Unfortunately, that other part of you—the part that would love to turn off the phone, play with the kids, clean the closet, avoid crowds, read a book, jog or walk through a local park, plant a garden—rarely, if ever, gets a chance to be nurtured. Your normal life keeps you way too busy, or you're on vacation away from home.

Kris and I had a great home based vacation several years ago. We agreed that work was off limits—even for one minute during the week. No work-related phone calls would be made or returned—just like we were on vacation. As far as we (and everyone else) were concerned, we *were* on vacation. We turned the ringer on the phone to the "off" position.

We hired a baby-sitter (the kids' favorite person, to make it fun for them) to play with the kids every morning for a few hours while we went jogging together, did yoga, or went out to breakfast. We did several little home projects we had wanted to do for years. We worked in the garden. We sat in the sun and read. It was heavenly. In the afternoons, we did something really fun as a family—hiking, swimming, or hide-and-seek. One day, we hired a massage therapist to give us back-to-back massages, and every night we had different take-out for dinner. We had someone come to the house and help us with the cleaning and laundry—just like being at a hotel. We saw several great movies and we slept in every day. It was like having nine Sundays back to back at a great hotel—at a tiny fraction of the cost!

The kids had a blast, and so did we. We felt as if we finally had the chance to really enjoy our home as a family. The kids were able to see their parents not rushed, at home. (What a concept!) I was more relaxed and rested than I ever remember being after going away for a vacation. And it was so much easier, not only to plan, but to get back into the swing of things once I was back—no travel delays, no lost bags, no jet lag, and no exhaustion from traveling with kids. Because we thought of it as a vacation, we lived like royalty that week—massages, restaurants, a house cleaner, take-out—yet we spent a fraction of what we would have spent flying or even driving to some exotic vacation or fancy hotel. But more than all of that, it was truly special. We realized we work so hard to have a home and to care for it—yet it's so rare that we get to enjoy it without being in a hurry.

I'm not advocating replacing all traditional vacations. I love to go away, and I suspect you do too. I can tell you, however, that this is a great way to relax, as well as a chance to do things you almost never get to do at or close to home, while spending very little money. As I look at my calendar, I can see that we have another one of these home vacations coming up soon. I can hardly wait.

78.

DON'T LET NEGATIVE COWORKERS
GET YOU DOWN

Regardless of where you work or what you do for a living, it's almost inevitable that you're going to have to deal with your share of negative people. Some of these people are going to have bad attitudes, others may be cynical or passive-aggressive, and some are probably going to be downright angry.

Learning to deal with negative people is a real art form, but I can tell you with absolute certainty that it's well worth the effort. Consider your options. If you don't learn the secrets of dealing effectively with negativity, then certainly there will be times when these people will bring you down with them. Their negativity will rub off on you, and you'll end up discouraged, frustrated, or even depressed. If you don't do what's necessary to deal gracefully with negative people, you may yourself end up cynical and negative.

You can get to a point where negative people rarely, if ever, bring you down. I believe that the best place to start is by increasing your level of compassion. It's critical to see the innocence, to understand that when someone is negative, they are unfulfilled or in some way unhappy. In most cases, they are not doing it on purpose. Like you, they would prefer to experience contentment and joy. They just don't know how.

Enthusiasm is our most natural state of being. In other words, it's natural to feel inspired, positive, creative, interested, and uplifted by the work that we choose to do. When this quality is lacking, something is wrong. So, when someone regularly expresses negativity, there is almost certainly something missing in that person's life. Their negative attitude and behavior are stemming from a sense of lack, a sense that something is wrong or out of place.

One of the reasons negativity tends to bring us down is that we take it personally or we feel that we are in some way responsible. When viewed with compassion, however, it's easy to see that negativity is usually not directed at us, even if it appears to be. Nor is it our fault.

Try to imagine (or remember) how horrible it feels to be negative and to lack enthusiasm. When you do, it will become clear that if a negative person felt that he or she had any realistic alternatives, they wouldn't be acting negatively. They certainly aren't doing it on purpose or for the fun of it.

Usually, only one of two possibilities will result when two people communicate or work together. Either the more negative person will lower the spirits of the more positive person, or the more positive person will somehow lift the spirits of the other. Your best chance of distancing yourself from the effects of negativity is to remain enthusiastic yourself, therefore being part of the solution rather than contributing to the problem. Instead of focusing on how hard it is to be around a negative person, or over-analyzing the reasons why the person is the way he is, try instead to be genuinely enthusiastic about your work and about your life in general. In all likelihood, you will have a significant effect on the negative people you work with. But, even if you don't, you'll be assured of being less adversely affected.

79.

MAKE THE BEST OF A
"NONCREATIVE" POSITION

I felt compelled to include this strategy because I've spoken to so many people over the years, who either complain about their "non-creative" position or yearn for a more interesting job.

Yet actually, you have a choice regarding any job that you might consider to be noncreative. You can dread each day, count the minutes, remind yourself again and again how boring your job is, complain and whine and wish it were different. Or, you can remind yourself, "It is what it is," and go ahead and make the best of it. You can smile, be enthusiastic, and have a positive attitude. You can find ways to make the job as interesting as it can possibly be. You'll be at work for the same number of hours, either way. In a year's time, you will likely have worked 2,000 hours, perhaps even more.

Once in a while I'll meet someone who will say, "Oh yeah, you haven't seen my job," meaning of course, that this advice doesn't apply in all situations. I beg to differ. In reality, you always have the choice to make the best of it or not.

There's a story I love about two bricklayers who were interviewed by a reporter. The reporter asked the first worker how he spent his day. He replied in a resentful tone, "I spend hours in the hot sun picking up these stupid bricks and putting them on top of each other. Leave me alone."

The reporter turned to the second worker and asked the same question. His response was quite different. He said in a grateful, enthusiastic tone, "I take these simple bricks and turn them into beautiful structures. Without people like me, there would be no buildings and no economy." The moral of the story is, of course, that both workers are correct—depending on how you look at it. I've met toll-takers who have told me that their job isn't to take money from people, but to see how many people they can make smile. I've seen popcorn and candy salespeople who entertain their customers as much as the professional ballplayers, always smiling and always evincing an uplifting attitude.

I've found that those people who approach their job in this positive way are almost always the ones who enjoy their work the most—and usually the ones who move quickly up the ladder if that is what they choose to do. Their attitude is lighthearted and relaxing to themselves, and inspiring and contagious to others.

Customers love these types of people, as do coworkers. They tend to use their lunch and other breaks to study, learn new things, or reflect on their dreams and how they are going to achieve them. They never feel victimized, almost always seek advice from experts, and are willing to listen to those who know the ropes. In every sense of the word, they understand that "it is what it is," and they definitely make the best of it. If you've gotten in the habit of thinking only certain jobs and careers can be fun, give it some more thought. When you make the best of it, almost anything can be "creative."

80.

STAY CLOSE
TO YOUR CENTER

Being centered lies at the heart of a satisfying, productive, and effective life. It's a quality that most people admire and many aspire to. It's a quality I have attempted to nurture for as long as I can remember, and it remains one of my top priorities. There's no question in my mind that any success and happiness I have achieved is a direct result of this quality. And as I look back on my life, it's clear that most of my troubles, failures, and major mistakes have been the result of losing my center and getting off-balance.

Your center is a calm, inspired feeling. When you're centered, you have the sense that you're flowing, on target, and in the groove. You have the feeling that you're on track, that you'll be able to work things out, solve your problems, and get your work done. Despite any apparent difficulties, you feel confident, enthusiastic, and in control. You're able to remain calm and collected in the eye of the storm. Even though you're not exerting tremendous effort, you have a healthy flow of thoughts that are organized and creative. Little things don't bug you.

On the other hand, when you're off-center, you are filled with frightened, scattered, agitated, and other stressful feelings. You tend to panic and assume the worst. You feel pressured and off-balance, as if there's not enough time. Being off-center brings with it feelings of being bothered and frenetic. There is a lack of concentration, and you're out of the flow. You're distracted, stressed, and more prone to making mistakes. Virtually everything bugs you.

You can think of your center as home base, your most natural way of being. Your center is built into your psyche in the same way that an ideal temperature is built into your body. In both cases, you can get off track, but your natural instinct is to return home. Because this is your most natural state of mind, there is nothing you have to do to get there. Rather, it's more a matter of knowing what not to do. In other words, in the absence of a busy, distracted mind, this is the state of mind you would be in most of the time, the feeling you would keep coming back to. Therefore, to return to your center, all you have to do is let go of your stressful thinking, and clear your mind. The rest takes care of itself.

Staying close to your center isn't as difficult as you might imagine. It involves paying attention to your feelings and gently bringing yourself back when you start to drift away. For example, you might be working on a project when your attention starts to drift forward in anticipation of your impending deadline. You begin to imagine the various responses to your work. You think to yourself, "I'll bet she won't approve of or appreciate what I've done."

If you pay attention to the feelings that accompany these thoughts, you'll probably notice yourself beginning to get tense and stressed. In moments like these, you're moving away from your center toward inner chaos and stress.

You're at an important fork in the road. If you continue with your train of thought, it's likely that you will continue to feel agitated, pressured, and maybe even resentful. If you observe what's happening, however, you'll notice that you can choose to back off your thinking for the moment in order to regain your bearings and get back closer to your center.

Built into your center is the wisdom you need to put all odds in your favor and to do everything possible to achieve your goals. In other words, the fact that you're not getting hysterical doesn't mean you're not going to meet your deadline and do a superb job. To the contrary, because you're centered and focused, you'll do a better job in far less time.

There's no question that staying close to your center is in your best interest. I encourage you to explore this idea, work with it, and enjoy the rewards.

81.

FORGIVE YOURSELF;
YOU'RE HUMAN

Earlier I mentioned the quote, "To err is human, to forgive divine." You might as well insert the word "yourself" into this all-so-true observation about being human. Let's face it. We are human, and to be human means you're going to make errors, at least some of the time. You're going to make plenty of mistakes, mess up from time to time, lose your way, forget things, lose your temper, say things you shouldn't have, and all the rest. I've never understood why this simple fact of life—our tendency to make mistakes— is so surprising or disappointing to people. I certainly don't understand why it's such a big deal.

To me, one of the saddest mistakes we make is a lack of forgiveness, especially to ourselves. We constantly remind ourselves of our flaws and previous mistakes. We anticipate future mistakes. We're highly critical of ourselves, frequently disappointed, and ruthless in our self-judgment. We badger and blame ourselves, and often we're our own worst enemy.

It seems to me that to be unforgiving of yourself is foolish and ridiculous. Life didn't come with a fool-proof manual. Most of us are doing the best that we can—really. But we're not perfect. The truth is, we're a work-in-progress. We learn from our mistakes and from stumbling. The best any of us can do, in any given moment, is to call it as we see it, to give it our best shot. None of us, however, certainly not I, have mastered life.

I'm sure that one of the reasons I'm a happy person is that I'm very forgiving of my mistakes. Someone recently asked me how I learned to be so kind to myself. My response was, "Because I've made so many mistakes, I've had lots of practice." She laughed, but it's actually true—I have had lots of practice! I can assure you, however, that my mistakes are not intentional. I truly do the best that I can. My work ethic as well as my standard of excellence is as high as most people's. So my forgiving attitude toward myself has nothing to do with any sort of apathy or a lowering of standards. It's more a matter of being realistic. Like almost everyone else, I have a great number of responsibilities. In fact, it usually seems like I'm juggling ten or twenty balls in the air simultaneously. So, to assume I'll never make mistakes is absurd.

Can you sense how framing mistakes in this more realistic way gets you off the hook? In other words, when you make a mistake—even a stupid one—this more philosophic outlook allows you to keep your perspective and sense of humor instead of beating yourself up. Instead of saying to yourself, "What an idiot," you'll be able to say, "More proof that I'm human."

Jack is a broker for a large financial institution. About a decade ago, a client specifically asked him to invest his life savings in a little stock called Intel! Jack, conservative by nature, convinced his client that it's never a good idea to invest in individual stocks, even at his client's relatively young age of 45. Jack felt it would be a better idea to put all the money in mutual funds.

Obviously, in this specific instance, Jack's advice cost his client a fortune. Jack had given the same advice to a number of other people, and he became despondent and self-destructive. He lost his self-confidence and eventually changed careers. All this because he simply couldn't forgive himself. His friends, colleagues, even his clients, tried to convince him that his judgment and rationale at the time were solid—and that, by most standards, his clients had all done exceptionally well. He should be proud. When someone is unforgiving of himself, however, logic isn't usually received with an open mind.

Luckily, at some point, he hooked up with a good therapist who taught him the obvious—that everything is much clearer in hindsight and that noone has a crystal ball. Eventually, he was able to forgive himself and return to the career he had loved—financial planning.

Obviously, some mistakes are big. An air-traffic control mistake or one wrong move by a surgeon can be deadly. A vast majority of the mistakes we make, however, are not life or death; they are nothing more than "small stuff" disguised as "big stuff." It's true that even small mistakes can cause inconvenience, conflict, or extra work—and, as in the previous example, can be expensive—but what else is new? When did life suddenly become convenient or trouble-free?

While no one enjoys making mistakes, there is something very freeing about learning to accept them—really accept them—as an unavoidable part of life. When we do, we can forgive ourselves, thus erasing all the stress that usually results from badgering ourselves. So my suggestion is simple. Forgive yourself; you're human.

82.

PUT YOUR MIND
IN NEUTRAL

One of the first observations I made when I learned to meditate was that my life seemed to calm down. Although I had the same number of things to do, the same responsibilities, and identical problems to deal with, I felt as if I had more time, which made my work life become easier and more enjoyable. I was still surrounded by chaos, but not as adversely affected by it.

While meditation isn't for everyone, there is a reasonable substitute that can be of tremendous help to anyone wishing to become calmer, less reactive, and more peaceful. It involves learning to put your mind in neutral, which you might think of as a form of "active meditation." In other words, unlike some forms of traditional meditation where you sit down, close your eyes, and focus on your breath, active meditation is something you can incorporate into your daily life. The truth is, there are select times you already engage in this process but because it doesn't seem like much, you probably disregard it as insignificant. Therefore, you never learn to use its power.

Essentially, putting your mind in neutral means clearing your mind of focused thinking. Rather than actively thinking, your mind is in a more passive or relaxed state. When your mind is in neutral, your experience of thought is effortless, yet completely responsive to whatever is happening in the moment. Great teachers, for example, or public speakers, will often describe "being on" or "being in the zone" as those times when their thinking is very relaxed, when they aren't forcing the issue.

My best writing is always produced when my mind is in neutral, when I'm not "trying." As I clear my mind, it's almost as though the writing is done for me. Rather than actively pursuing ideas, the thoughts I need and the best ways to express them come to me or "through me." You may notice that when you suddenly remember an important phone number, a person's name, or a forgotten combination, or when you suddenly have an idea that solves a problem, or when you remember where you put your keys, it's your usually relaxed "neutral thinking" that provides the insight or sudden surge of memory. You'll have a "That's it!" moment. At times like these, the harder you try, the less is achieved. It's this effortless quality that is so critical and helpful. Once you start trying or focusing your thinking, you put yourself back into your more normal or analytical thinking.

The reason most people don't consciously use neutral thinking is because they don't recognize its power, or necessarily even consider it to be a form of thinking—but it is. It's taken for granted, seldom used, and almost always overlooked. However, although it's relaxing and de-stressing, it's also very powerful. When your mind is in neutral, thoughts seem to come to you as if out of the blue. New ideas and insights become a way of life because your mind, when it's relaxed, becomes open and receptive to your wisdom and unique greatness.

Obviously, there are times when it's inappropriate or impractical to put your mind in neutral. When your task requires focused concentration, or when you're learning something brand new, it's often in your best interest to think in a more traditional, analytical mode. You'll be amazed, however, at how powerful this process really is—and how much easier your life can become when you learn to incorporate neutral thinking into your daily life. Whenever you feel highly stressed or as though you're expending too much mental energy, it's a good idea to check in with yourself and decide if a little neutral thinking might be just what you need. You can use neutral thinking as a stress-reducing tool, as a way to relax, or as a way to bring forth greater creativity. The applications are virtually unlimited.

To put your mind in neutral is surprisingly simple. You can only be in one mode of thinking or the other—neutral or active. Like a walkie-talkie, you are either on "talk" or "listen," but never both at the same time. So, as you let go or back off of your analytical thinking, your mind automatically shifts into neutral. Once you accept neutral as a viable form of thinking, the rest is easy. I hope you'll experiment with backing off your thinking and quieting your mind. Soon you'll be more relaxed than you could have ever imagined.

83.

MARVEL AT HOW OFTEN
THINGS GO RIGHT

If you were to eavesdrop on a typical conversation and if you took what you heard to heart, it would be easy to believe that almost nothing ever goes right! The focus of many conversations is limited to, or at least slanted toward, the problems of the day, the ills of society, the obstacles, injustices, and the hassles of work. The emphasis is almost always on the negative or on what's wrong. There's a great deal of discussion of what's wrong with other people, coworkers, customers, investors, clients, and everyone else. The working environment is criticized, and nothing is ever quite good enough.

But have you ever, even once, stopped to marvel at just how often things go right? It's amazing. Literally thousands of events—work related and otherwise—go right every single day, without a glitch. Everything from the vast majority of phone calls that are returned and reservations that are honored, to travel and food safety, dependency on various forms of technology, roofs that don't leak, the competency of coworkers, the interdependence of schedules, right down to the fact that most people are friendly—so much goes right. And for the most part, we take it all for granted. For whatever reasons, we choose to focus on the few exceptions. Perhaps we believe that more will go right if we focus on what's wrong. Conversely, many people are frightened that if they were to become more accepting of imperfection, then more things would end up going wrong—which isn't true.

I fly quite a bit and hear a great deal of complaining about air travel. And it's true that I've had a few horrible experiences pertaining to delays, canceled flights, lost or missing baggage, overbooking, misplaced reservations, and other hassles. However, the percentage of the time that I get where I need to go either on time or nearly on time is astonishing. Given the enormous amount of traffic volume, tight schedules, weather conditions, and dependency on technology, this is truly remarkable. For example, I can wake up in Northern California and before dinner, I'm safely in New York City, baggage in hand—most of the time. I suspect that similar percentages of good fortune are true for most business travelers.

Yet have you ever heard anyone complimenting the airlines? I'm sure that if you have, it's been the exception, rather than the norm. In the midst of a delay, we're far more inclined to become angry and frustrated, maybe even take it personally, than we are to keep in mind that everyone involved is doing the very best he or she can, and that occasional delays are inevitable. The same lack of perspective seems to be true with so many aspects of daily business. A huge percentage of people are friendly, helpful, and courteous. What you hear about, however, are the tiny percentage of people who are rude, insensitive or incompetent. A person may have a dozen tasks to complete in a day. Eleven of them went smoothly; the other one is discussed over dinner.

I'm not going to discount the fact that there are problems to deal with; there most certainly are. Likewise, most of us must face our share of hassles, disappointments, incompetence, and rejection. It's all part of working for a living. It seems that we've become so accustomed to things going smoothly, however, that we expect near-perfection. When we don't get it, we go crazy.

I think it's wise to keep at least a little bit of perspective. When I remind myself of how often things actually go right, it really helps me deal with those things that don't. It allows me to make allowances for the fact that "stuff happens," people make errors, Mother Nature does her thing, and things do sometimes go wrong. What else is new? When I focus on how often things go right, it opens my eyes to the bigger picture and keeps me from sweating the small stuff. I think the same will be true for you as well.

84.

MAKE PEACE WITH CHAOS

One of my favorite "to the point" quotes is from Wallace Stegner. It has helped me immensely in my efforts to keep things in perspective. It reads, "Chaos is the law of nature. Order is the dream of man." Reminding myself of these words has brought me great comfort during times of extreme stress and disorder, as well as in my daily work life. They have given me perspective when I have needed it most.

Indeed, chaos is the law of nature. It's everywhere you look. People are coming and going, trends come and go, there are unlimited conflicting interests and desires, and change is constant and inevitable. Phones are ringing, demands and requests are being made of you, and piles of paper are always on your desk. Even though you try to be fair, you sometimes end up being a hero to one person and someone else's enemy—without even knowing why. A plan unfolds, another falls apart. One person gets a promotion and is thrilled; someone else is laid off, devastated and angry. You try to help, but only make matters worse. People are confused, frustrated, and stressed-out. Just when you think you're about to get on top of things, you catch a cold!

Despite this undeniable law of nature, human beings would love to have at least some degree of order. We would love to be able to keep things the same, predict our future, keep a perfect balance, and know the answers. But no one can make perfect sense of chaos because it doesn't really make any sense—it just exists. Indeed, no matter how hard you try, chaos is right beside you.

There is something magical that happens to you, however, when you surrender to chaos—when you make peace with it. By easing up on your need to control your environment or predict certain outcomes, you're able to learn to work within an environment of chaos without being as affected by it. You begin to experience chaos with a degree of equanimity, with a sense of humor and perspective.

The trick seems to lie in the willingness to embrace rather than struggle against the chaos. In other words, surrendering to the way things really are instead of insisting that things be a certain way. We must come to peace with the fact that chaos is a law of nature—just like gravity. The quality of surrender allows you to look at chaos in a new way. Rather than being caught off-guard and annoyed when you see it, you'll be able to say, "There it is again." You'll acknowledge it and respect the fact that it exists, but not be defeated by it. Rather than fighting against it, you'll be able to choose the path of least resistance.

Allison works evenings in a hospital emergency room. I asked her what chaos meant to her. "Sometimes, every minute is like a nightmare. Someone is rushed in who has been shot—side by side with someone who has been involved in a serious auto accident. Sometimes we have to prioritize that which shouldn't have to be prioritized. People are in pain. There is panic, disorder, concern and tears. Who are you supposed to help first when everyone wants and needs you, all at the same time? We have policies, of course, but they don't always apply or seem fair. It often seems that I'm being yelled at by someone, and rarely is there time to catch my breath. But, despite all the chaos, I've learned to keep my cool—at least most of the time. You have to, or you'd go crazy and, more importantly, the patients' care would suffer." Her description helped me to put that which I perceive as chaos into better perspective.

To a lesser extent than Allison, I have learned to accept chaos as an inevitable part of life. I still don't like it, and I do everything I can to avoid it and keep it to a minimum. Yet, by surrendering to it, I've made peace with the fact that chaos is inevitable. Life isn't as predictable, as organized, or as hassle-free as I would prefer. Instead, it's just the way it is.

I've accepted this, and the results have been astonishing. Many of the same potentially frustrating things happen in my day-to-day life—unreturned phone calls, lost mail, miscalculations, mistakes, overcommitments, deadlines, disapproval, and all the rest. The difference, however, is in the way they affect me, or more accurately, the way they *don't* affect me. Many things that used to drive me crazy are now seen for what they are—just another part of the chaos. I've found that there are enough challenges in life to contend with, without also fighting and struggling against things that can't be controlled or avoided. Chaos is on top of this list. Perhaps you, too, can open your heart to chaos and accept it for what it is. If you do, you'll notice far fewer things getting to you.

85.

PREVENT BURNOUT

Work-related burnout is an enormous, disruptive, and often expensive problem for millions of people. To put it bluntly, people get sick of and fed up with their jobs and crave a better, different, or more satisfying life. Obviously, there's no way to guarantee the prevention of burnout, but there are things you can do to put the odds in your favor.

The keys seem to be balance and growth. If you talk to people who aren't burned out, you'll discover that most of them strive to have a balanced life and to be growth-oriented. This means that while they work hard, compete well, strive for excellence, and have very specific, often lofty goals, they nevertheless insist on having a life outside of work—they enjoy and spend time with their families and friends, they exercise or enjoy hobbies, they value their free time, and strive to make a contribution to their community apart from their work. In addition, people who avoid burnout are constantly attempting to better themselves and to grow, not just professionally, but spiritually and emotionally as well. They attend workshops or classes, they learn new things, and are open-minded. They strive to overcome their own blind spots. They have a fascination with learning and a zest for life. They are curious and enjoy listening to others.

Those who avoid burnout do so with their uplifting, positive attitude. They have outside interests and take advantage of their time away from work. Their interest in and ability to focus on aspects of life other than work keeps their spirits nourished and their lives relatively content. Doesn't it make sense that if a person was fulfilled and satisfied outside of work, he would carry that sense of freshness and wonder into his work life?

When all you do is work, even if it's satisfying, burnout will be the end result. You're too invested in one thing. You become stagnant, predictable, habitual, even boring. Think about it. What would happen if you only ate one food, over and over again, day after day, year after year? It wouldn't matter if it was your favorite food or not—you'd get sick of it. Or what if you watched the same episode of your favorite television show again and again? Boring!

Andrew worked for the same mid-sized company for fifteen years before he caught a major case of burnout. Outside of work, he had no life to speak of—no exercise or outside activities, very few friends (and almost no time spent with them), no pets, and no real hobbies. Because his whole world was his job, he assumed that his job was the source of his burnout. He didn't know what to do. Eventually, he became so frustrated, he resigned.

He didn't have the financial luxury of *not* working for too long, so, within a month or so, he was forced to start looking for a new job. During his month off, however, he tried some new things for the first time—and loved them. He read a few books, took some regular walks, and even enrolled in a yoga class. "I not only had fun but met some really nice and interesting people too," he told me. For the first time in his life, he was having fun. His enthusiasm returned, his burnout disappeared and his perspective was enhanced.

Because he felt so much better, he called his old boss and explained what had happened. Luckily for Andrew, his company hadn't found an adequate replacement and they offered him his old job back—which he accepted with gratitude. He realized that there was nothing wrong with his career, but that his life lacked balance. He made the commitment to keep doing the things he now knew he enjoyed and, in fact, to try even more things as time went on.

This is a strategy that some (really busy) people try to dismiss with the old excuse, "I don't have time to have a life." Unfortunately, this is a narrow, shallow, and extremely short-term way of looking at your life and your career. The truth is for most people, if you don't "get a life," you will end up with a major case of burnout. You're playing with fire—it's only a matter of time. So, you have to ask yourself, "Is it smarter for me (i.e., better business) to continue my lopsided, out-of-balance lifestyle, or might it be better to reserve even a little time for some other things—regular reading, exercise, meditation, an evening with friends, time alone or with family, a course on how to have a positive attitude, or some hobby?"

Even if you're a full-fledged workaholic, or if you are by circumstances forced to work excessive hours, it's a great idea to at least think of balance as a desirable goal. But hard as it can be, you must back up your good intentions with action.

A good place to start is to evaluate your priorities apart from work. If you had to pick, what would be most important? Would it be to volunteer some time or learn to meditate? Is it your spiritual life that's most important? Would it be to schedule a regular date with your partner, child or friend? Or might it be to exercise on a regular basis—or something else entirely? Whatever it is, take a look at your calendar and begin to carve out the time. Anything is better than nothing.

I remember when I began running on a regular basis. The only realistic time for me to do it was early in the morning, well before sunrise. So that's when I did it. Some health clubs are open twenty-four hours a day. Where there is a will, there's a way. Perhaps you can volunteer some time on the weekends, as I used to do for the Big Brothers of America program, or set aside thirty minutes each evening to relax in the bathtub and read a great novel.

Most people take a lunch break. You can spend this time watching a soap opera in the lunch room or learning to meditate. It's your choice. If you work five days a week, a year from now you will have had 260 lunch breaks. In that time alone, you could be well on your way to speaking a foreign language, being in better physical condition, becoming semiproficient in yoga, or many other worthwhile ventures. Whatever it is that you love to do, it will be worth it, and it will help you create a more balanced, growth-oriented life. It's inconceivable that you wouldn't feel better about life and about yourself by creating some balance. And as an added bonus, you'll prevent burnout. It really is that simple.

86.

EXPERIENCE A MAGICAL
TRANSFORMATION

If you're looking for a way to jolt yourself out of being stuck or to give yourself a fresh start, this strategy may help. A magical transformation is like a new beginning. It involves extricating yourself from an old, worn-out way of thinking or behaving, and replacing it with a more positive alternative. The transformation itself occurs out of the blue, often when you least expect it. In a way, the experience is like learning to ride a bike. One minute you can't do it—and the next you can.

Magical transformations can occur in many ways and might be the result of any number of issues you are facing. It might involve giving up a destructive habit or addiction, or it might be a matter of recognizing a self-defeating pattern of behavior or attitude and somehow seeing how to change it.

The easiest way to experience a transformation is to mentally review your most negative traits and habits, the ones you know you'd like to change, and to make a mental note that you'd like to see it differently. If you drink too much, for example, you might wish to experience a magical transformation and become a nondrinker. If you're always running late, you may wish to become a person who gives himself a little extra time. If you tend to be impatient, perhaps you'd like to become someone who is known for her patience. I was once sitting with a man who, in the midst of our conversation, had the sudden realization that he was virtually always critical. It was as if he saw it for the first time. I remember him saying, "I can't believe I've always been that way." From one extreme to another, magical transformations contribute to a changed life. It's as if you have a sudden shift upward in your level of understanding. They seem to occur most often shortly after you tell yourself you'd like to see things in a new way.

These positive transformations are life changing, not only because of your isolated shift in perspective, but also because they reinforce your resiliency, your ability to bounce back and change. Someone who is habitually frenetic who becomes genuinely calm tucks away this transformation into his memory. Then whenever he feels discouraged, he remembers this experience as validation of his strength and his ability to make changes. Once you experience a magical transformation, your sense of confidence in yourself will be enhanced.

I've had a number of these transformations during my lifetime, and I hope to have many more. One, in particular, stands out in my mind.

Like most people, I was very sensitive to criticism. When someone would make a suggestion or criticize me in some way, I would feel attacked. Usually, I would act or at least feel defensive. I would defend my ground and my actions.

About fifteen years ago I had an instant change of heart, or magical transformation. I was standing in my kitchen with my back turned when some heavy criticism was thrown in my direction. My initial instinct was to coil up and defend myself. My thoughts began to spin and churn, as they had always done before. But for some reason, I recognized my own mental contribution to the problem and, for the first time in my life, I realized that I had a genuine choice in how I was going to respond and in fact, how I was going to feel.

I could see myself as the thinker of my own thoughts. In other words, I recognized that although the critical comment was directed at me, it was now in my court, and only my own thinking could keep the experience alive in my mind. Without my consent, the comment had no power! The metaphor that came to me was that of a check—it's not worth anything unless it's signed. In the same way, in order to feel hurt by criticism, I have to take the bait.

For the first time in my life I was able to dismiss the comment and go on with my day—no hurt feelings, defensive behavior, or retaliation. I wasn't pretending that it didn't hurt—it really didn't. The comment was made and I let it go. I had experienced my first magical transformation and to this day, I'm seldom bothered by criticism. Obviously, my experience is only one out of an unlimited number of possibilities. Yours will be unique.

Experiencing a magical transformation involves recognizing that you do, indeed, have a choice. I wanted to share this story and this strategy because so often, once you are aware that magical transformations are possible, you begin to look for them in your own life. When you're frustrated, for example, you might find yourself saying something like, "I know it's possible to see this (or experience this) differently." And often, this awareness or even hope that there is another way of experiencing your conflict, dilemma, or problem opens the door for it to occur. I hope that by opening to the possibility, you too will have a magical transformation.

87.

AVOID "IF ONLY, THEN" THINKING

I first began reflecting on this idea more than twenty years ago. It has always struck me how often many of us fall into this tendency, or mental habit, that virtually guarantees a great deal of stress and a lack of satisfaction. As I have reflected on this concept, and as I have engaged in this habit less often in my own life, I've found that my stress level is substantially lower than it once was. I have also noticed that I truly enjoy virtually everything that I do that is related to my work. In the process, I have also become more effective. I hope that you can realize the same types of benefits by becoming more familiar with this concept and by putting it into practice in your own life.

Just as it sounds, "if only, then" thinking refers to the oh-so-common tendency to fill your head with thoughts designed to convince yourself that "if only" certain conditions were met—then you'd be happy (or satisfied, or less stressed, or peaceful, or whatever). It's a form of longing, or imagining that if things were different, boy-oh-boy would things be great! Here are a few examples of what could be a very long list: "If only I made more money, then I'd feel secure," "If only I received more attention or credit, then I'd feel good," "If only he (or she) were different, I'd have a better life," "If only I could go on a certain vacation, then I could relax," "If only I could make some headway on this in-basket, then I'd spend some time with the kids," " If only I could live in a larger home, then I'd feel satisfied." You get the picture.

In order to see the flaw in "if only, then" thinking, all you need to do is think back to a few of the thousands of times you told yourself essentially the same thing, and ended up getting exactly what you wanted, and you still weren't satisfied. Or if you were, it didn't last for long! You convinced yourself that if only you could get that new car, you'd feel great. But a day or two after getting it, the thrill was gone. You told yourself that a new relationship would fulfill your every need, yet when you found that "perfect person," you inevitably found that you struggled with him (or her) too. You make more money than you used to, yet despite telling yourself how secure you'd feel when you did, you still worry and want even more.

This type of thinking is destructive to the human spirit because longing to be somewhere else, or to be doing something else, or to have different circumstances is almost by definition stressful. It's almost like saying, "I'm going to put my happiness on hold. I'll be happy later, once things change." How often do you forget to appreciate the life you already have because you are too busy thinking about how grateful you will be somewhere down the road? It's almost impossible to be content when you're focused on future plans because your mind isn't engaged in the moment, but focused elsewhere.

Obviously, I'm not suggesting that you don't have to know where you're going or that it's not important to have a plan. You probably do, and it is. Neither am I saying you don't have to work hard to achieve your goals. You do. What I'm talking about here is the tendency to discredit or under-acknowledge the life you have now at the expense of some imagined future. So, whether you're an entrepreneur, work for someone else, or are climbing the corporate ladder, don't forget to enjoy and absorb yourself in every step along the way. Keep in mind that happiness is a journey, not a destination. My dad used to say to me, "If you start out at the bottom, enjoy it while you can. Because if you do, you won't be there for long." What I've found is that his words of wisdom are true in whatever you do for a living. When you are fully engaged and make the best of what you are doing, you will bring out the best in yourself.

My advice is simple. Go ahead and be all you can be, dream your dreams, and have a plan. But never forget that the secret to satisfaction isn't getting to some imagined destination, but in enjoying the ride along the way.

88.

ELIMINATE THE WORRY FACTOR

Those of you who are familiar with my work may be aware that because it's such a destructive force in the lives of so many people, worry is one of my favorite subjects to tackle. In fact, my entire book *Don't Worry, Make Money* is dedicated to overcoming this often insidious tendency. In it, I make the connection between less worry and more success.

For our purposes here, there are several additional reasons to eliminate worry from your life. First and foremost, it's highly stressful. Think about how you feel when you're worried. It's all-consuming and energy-draining. It encourages you to focus on problems and on how difficult your life has become. When you worry, you are on edge and tense. Therefore you tend to be easily bothered or irrationally upset—the perfect conditions for sweating the small stuff.

When you worry, it's more difficult to concentrate and focus your efforts. Rather than being completely absorbed in your work, your mind tends to wander toward an uncertain future or a mistake-ridden past. You anticipate trouble, whether it's realistic or not—and you review past mistakes as a way to justify your concerns.

For example, you might be worried about an upcoming review of your work by your employer. Rather than giving your job your undivided attention, you spend the week prior to your review thinking and worrying about the possible consequences. You remember the negative highlights of your last job review. Your mind drifts and your thinking is scattered.

Instead of being as highly productive and efficient as you usually are, your work suffers and you become more insecure. Obviously, this insecurity and the accompanying less-than-ideal performance will be noticed by your employer and possibly reflected in your review. It's a vicious cycle that begins with worry.

Worry is also contagious. When you worry, it either suggests or reinforces the idea (to others) that there is something legitimate to worry about. It spreads a negative message and a feeling of fear. This feeds into an overly cautious, sometimes even paranoid working environment. When people are frightened, it sets the stage for selfish and narcissistic behavior where self-protection is the first priority.

Ellen, an ex-big-time worrier, manages a large florist. She told me she used to worry all the time, especially about large events such as weddings. She told me of one specific example when she finally realized she had to change.

She and three others were preparing for a large wedding. To date, this was one of their largest orders, and she was worrying more than usual. She feared she had written the order down incorrectly and she felt certain that there was no way they would have the complete order done in time. She just knew something major was going to go wrong. She was rushing around, visibly shaken, when she finally realized that the others were doing the exact same thing. They were making obvious mistakes, knocking over vases, cutting in the wrong places and every other mistake a florist might make. Ellen told me, "It was so bad, I just had to laugh out loud." It was obvious that her nervousness and sense of worry was indeed contagious—and that everyone around her had caught it, too. Ellen took her colleagues out for a coffee break, where everyone loosened up and relaxed. When they got back to the shop, they proceeded with their normal efficiency, not getting overly stressed about the order—and the arrangements came out perfectly.

A powerful, internal shift begins to take place as you lose your respect for worry. A new type of trust develops within yourself. In a very practical way, you begin to trust that in the absence of worry, you'll know exactly what to do and you'll know how to go about it.

An ideal example of this process exists in the field of public speaking. You can spend years worrying and telling yourself how hard it is to speak to large groups of people. You can anticipate the worst and play it out in your mind. And every time you try, you're even more convinced because your fear is validated by your negative experience.

Yet many speakers will tell you, as I will now, that you won't stop worrying by having good experiences—as much as you will have good experiences by letting go of worry. It's one of those "put the cart before the horse" issues. In other words, when you decide to throw caution to the wind and set your worry aside, you'll miraculously discover that speaking to a group is not all that different from speaking to a single person. In the absence of worry, you'll know what to say and you'll be responsive to the subject matter and the needs of the group. The same internal process occurs regardless of what you do for a living—get rid of the interference of worry, and your wisdom will surface.

Please understand that when I say "throw caution to the wind," I don't mean you stop caring, or that you become indifferent to the outcome. I'm merely suggesting that you become aware of how credible and competent you are when you let go of the interfering and distracting aspects of worry. I encourage you to see for yourself how brilliant and resourceful you can be when you let go of worry. As this happens, your life will begin to seem easier and less stressful.

89.

ASK FOR WHAT YOU WANT, BUT
DON'T INSIST ON GETTING IT

There's an old saying: "If you don't ask for what you want, you're not going to get it." And while this isn't always the case, from a certain perspective it does make a great deal of sense. After all, if your boss doesn't know you want a raise or that you feel you deserve one, you can't really blame her for not extending the offer. Or if you'd like to have lunch with someone or pick their brain for ideas, chances are, it probably won't happen if you don't ask. If you're selling something, it's usually a good idea to ask for the sale—you certainly increase the odds.

The only problem with the "be willing to ask" philosophy is that it doesn't take into consideration the large percentage of the time that you don't get something, even when you do ask or when you feel you deserve it. So, the old saying, if taken literally, can create some frustration.

Any potential frustration, however, can be prevented by including a lack of insistence upon your desired result. In other words, it's terrific, courageous, and important to ask for what you want, but if you're attached to the outcome, you could be in for a long and ongoing series of disappointments in your life. You'll only be happy when you get exactly what you want and when life accommodates you with your preferences. Once you detach from the outcome, however, you'll win either way. You'll either get what you want—or you'll be okay with the fact that you didn't.

The key to becoming less attached to the outcomes of your requests is to depersonalize them. In other words, try to see that more often than not, being turned down has very little to do with you. For example, if you ask for a raise, your request may or may not be possible, depending on factors other than you—your company's budget, the implications to other workers, rules within the department, and so forth. Similarly, if you ask for a sale, you're more likely to get it. However, it's obviously the case that your customer may not want or be able to afford what you're selling.

Dennis, an accountant who worked for a grocery chain, loved his job except for one thing—the location of his office. His office was upstairs in the middle of the building. He told me, "It wasn't too bad, but it had no window. I felt I would work better if I had natural light." The problem was, there were only a few offices that had windows.

Dennis decided to act. He asked his boss what it would take to ever be allowed to change offices. He told him, gently, that he loved and appreciated his job, but that he has a tendency to get a little claustrophobic. He made it clear that it wasn't a "deal breaker," but that he would surely appreciate it if could be worked out. A week or two later, he wrote a thank-you note to his boss for listening to his concern and for taking it into consideration. The letter wasn't written with any edge or demands— just a simple note.

When I last spoke to Dennis, he still hadn't been moved. He did say, however, that he felt fine about it. He had done everything he could. The good news was that his boss had brought it up on several occasions and had said that, should something open up, he *would* get the new office. Dennis felt confident that, eventually, he would indeed have a window. I loved his story because it shows how it's possible to not get what you want (at least right away), and still feel good about it. It demonstrates the wisdom of asking for what you want—but not always insisting on it.

I've written or called hundreds of people during my career who have never written back or returned my call. I've learned that people are often overwhelmed and overcommitted, and therefore unable or unwilling to help me. Instead of feeling defeated, I try to focus instead on how grateful I am that many other people have returned my calls or answered my letters. I've learned that if it's in the cards, it happens. If not, that's okay too. The key to success is to keep trying, stay out there, but to detach from the outcome.

Sometimes it's helpful to put yourself in the shoes of the person you are asking. Many years ago, I wanted to get in to see a certain professional and was told that I couldn't because he wasn't taking any new clients. I persisted, but never succeeded. Finally, I spoke to the receptionist in an impatient tone and said, "Look, I really need to see him. Isn't there anything you can do?" She responded to me in a very calm and respectful manner. Her words were, "I'm truly sorry, Mr. Carlson, but the doctor has a three-year waiting list. He works six days a week, twelve hours a day, and hasn't had a vacation in over five years. He's doing the best he can, but he too would like to have a life." His schedule put my own busyness into better perspective.

When you're willing to ask for what you want but don't insist on getting it, there are some potential hidden benefits as well. For example, you sometimes bring out the compassion and generosity in others. Several years ago I arrived in Atlanta very late one evening. Despite having a confirmed reservation, the hotel was overbooked and was turning people away. The man in front of me was enraged and became very threatening.

He insisted on getting his way—but there were no rooms. He stormed out, defeated and angry. He was totally oblivious and insensitive to the fact that it wasn't the receptionist's fault. It wasn't personal.

I walked up to the receptionist and in a gentle voice I said, "I understand your predicament and don't blame you a bit. These things happen. I would appreciate it so much if you would help me. I know you don't have any rooms here, but could you help me find another hotel, close by?" I thought it was wise to ask—as long as I didn't insist. (I had just been reminded of how much good the insisting does.)

She was very nice and apologetic. Remarkably, she said she had some great news. She had completely overlooked the fact that one of the guests had to leave in an emergency and wouldn't be back. It turned out to be the largest and most expensive suite in the hotel! Because I had been so patient, she gave it to me at the lower rate.

The question is, why didn't she remember this empty room and give it to the angry man in front of me? He was there before I was, and seemed a lot more desperate for the room. I think the answer is pretty obvious. His insistence pushed her away and may have even contributed to her "forgetfulness." When I was talking to her, however, she relaxed and felt less pressure. Her memory returned and I ended up getting a few hours of much-needed sleep. So be sure to ask for what you want, but don't insist on getting it.

90.

REMEMBER THE WHOLE STORY

I predict that if you experiment with this strategy, you'll begin to realize that in most cases, your life isn't quite as bad as you can sometimes make it out to be. This in turn will heighten your perspective and enjoyment surrounding your work, and help you relax and reduce your stress.

As you probably know, it's extremely seductive, when sharing with others about your workday, to focus primarily on the negative. A fairly typical response to the question, "How was your day?" is, "I had a really tough one." If you elaborate, it's likely that you'll focus on how little time you had, your nightmare commute, the tough issues and conflicts, problems, difficult people, hassles, your sense of hurry and being rushed, negative coworkers, all the things that went wrong, and your demanding boss. And to a certain degree, you're probably right on the mark. For most people, a typical workday is really tough and often downright exhausting. But is this negative assessment the whole story—or is it only part of it? Are you recharacterizing your day the way it actually was—or are you being selective in what you choose to remember and discuss?

I encourage you to be completely honest with yourself as you ponder the following questions about your latest workday: On your way to work, did you stop for a bagel and coffee? Did you take a lunch break? If so, who were you with? Was it enjoyable? How was the food? Did you have any stimulating conversations during the day? Any new insights? Did you have a chance to express your creativity? Did you see any pretty sights or nature—a waterfall in your courtyard, trees and flowers, birds or animals? Did you hear any good jokes today? Did anyone give you a compliment? Did you listen to any good music in the car or perhaps an interesting talk show? Did your in-basket get any smaller? Did you resolve any conflicts? Are you being paid?

I'm not trying to get you to become unrealistically happy. As I mentioned above, I'm well aware that work can be (and often is) difficult. Yet let's not forget that if you answered any of the questions above with a positive response, your day was brighter than a vast majority of the world's population. This doesn't mean you should pretend that you had a wonderful day—yet isn't it easy to take the nice parts of your day completely for granted? We treat them as if they never happened, as if we had no perks, simple pleasures, or conveniences. Indeed, when you examine the above questions, it becomes clear that, for most of us, our day is not entirely negative—or even close to it. If this is the case, why do we describe it as such?

I think there are several reasons. First of all, many of us want to either impress others with our busyness or difficult life, or we are seeking sympathy. Rarely will you hear either spouse say to each other after a long day at work, "I had a terrific day. Lots of things went right." The fear is that to do so (even if it were true) might be seen as a weakness—as if your life were too easy. I know for a fact that some men complain to their wives about how difficult their workday is, in part, because they don't want to be expected to do too much once they get home!

In addition, most of us want to be appreciated and respected for how hard we work. By sharing all that went right during the day, the fear is that we might lose some of that appreciation or respect, and be taken for granted.

But more than all of that, focusing on the negative is just a bad habit—plain and simple. Complaining is contagious, and everyone seems to do it. So, unless you make a conscious effort to do less of it, you're probably going to continue for as long as you are working.

Since I began focusing more on the best parts of my day, my eyes have been opened to a whole new world. I've become increasingly aware that there are all sorts of interesting and enjoyable aspects to my day that were virtually invisible to me prior to this shift in focus. I no longer take for granted those stimulating conversations, interesting challenges, personal contact with friends and others. Perhaps most of all, my appreciation has been heightened. Because of this, I find myself less bothered and annoyed by the hassles and all the "small stuff" that I must deal with on a daily basis. I'm sure the same will be true for you.

91.

TAP INTO YOUR SECRET
STRESS-BUSTER

Many years ago I was home one night scrambling to finish a work-related project that was due the next day. I was uptight, stressed, hurried, and agitated. In those days, it seemed like I was always nervous about something.

A friend of mine who was considerably calmer and wiser was visiting from out of town. In his customary casual style, he looked at me very compassionately and said, "Richard, are you breathing?" Shocked and a little annoyed by what I believed to be a superficial question, I replied, "Of course I'm breathing, aren't you?"

He went on to explain that in his experience, most adults breathe too shallowly and do not get enough air into their lungs. He put his hand on my chest and showed me what I was doing (or wasn't doing). It was one of the most surprising moments of my life. I realized that I was breathing so superficially, it was almost as if I weren't breathing at all!

To my great surprise, as I began to take slightly deeper breaths, I felt instantly better. My body seemed to relax and my thinking became clearer. As I have become more practiced and a little better at taking deeper breaths, I've also noticed that I have more energy and, perhaps more than anything else, I almost never feel panicked the way I used to.

I'm not an expert in this area, but I have learned to breathe more deeply over the years. And although I can't prove it, I know in my heart that doing so has played a significant role in my own journey of becoming a less-stressed person. I'll bet that if you put a tiny bit of attention on the way you breathe, you may decide that it's in your best interest to learn to breathe a little deeper. In fact, you may be shocked at how quickly you can make an improvement in the way you feel and in the quality of your life.

The idea of breathing a little deeper makes sense if you think about it. After all, if you're really scared to do something, but you have to do it, what do you do? You may not even be aware of it, but you probably take a really deep breath. Have you ever seen a professional basketball player right before he or she shoots an important, pressure-packed free-throw? In most instances, the athlete takes a long, deep breath before taking the shot. What I'm suggesting in this strategy is that you incorporate deeper breathing into your everyday work life. Rather than waiting until you feel desperate to take a deep breath, why not instead take deeper breaths as a regular practice?

If you think about it, it's somewhat obvious. We're all rushing around like little bees, getting all sorts of things done. Yet if you aren't getting enough air in your lungs, is it any wonder most of us feel so panicked so much of the time? Taken to an extreme, it's as if we're suffocating. If you've ever been under water just a little too long, you know how paranoid and frightened you can become. In a way, when we aren't breathing deeply enough, it's as if we're all spending our workdays underwater—at least some of the time. True, we aren't going to drown, but we may pay an enormous price in terms of self-created stress.

Check in with your breath. How deep is your inhalation? Notice what happens when you consciously breathe just a little deeper. If you're like me, you'll instantly feel more relaxed and less stressed. When you're getting enough air, the world seems a little less crazy and things are brought into perspective. Life seems to move at a more manageable pace and many of those everyday annoyances don't seem to bother us quite as much. In a nutshell, you're less likely to sweat the small stuff if your body is getting enough air!

I think of my breathing as my own secret weapon that I can use against stress at any time. It's simple, produces quick and significant results, and is completely private. No one other than myself ever has to know that I'm breathing a little deeper in an attempt to relax. I hope you'll add this "weapon" to your arsenal against the stress in your work life. It's certainly helped me, and I'll bet it will help you too.

92.

SPEAK TO OTHERS WITH
LOVE AND RESPECT

Not too long ago, I was being interviewed by an extraordinary person who, off the air, shared with me a simple yet life-shaping story that he said contributed to his gentle, kind manner. I asked him if I could share his story and he said that I could.

Some twenty years ago, this man had bought a brand-new car with an area in the back that would accommodate his large, furry dog. Not too long after purchasing the car, he had it washed in an upscale, expensive car wash. Afterward, however, he noticed that the back portion of the car was still filled with dog hair. Because he had paid so much money for the wash, he felt ripped off and became upset.

He complained to the staff, but to no avail. They insisted that their policy was to "not vacuum the trunk." Apparently, they considered his "dog space" to be a trunk and therefore refused to do the extra work. When it became apparent that his complaining wasn't going to help, he demanded to see the manger.

He spent the next five minutes yelling at and chewing out the manager of the car wash in what he described as a harsh, obnoxious and arrogant tone. When he had finished his rampage, the manager looked him in the eye and in a gentle, undefensive tone, asked the man if he were finished. He said that he was.

The manager then told the customer in a calm, unthreatening tone that he would go ahead and vacuum the car himself until every dog hair was gone. Then, in a compassionate but firm voice, he said, "I have to ask you, sir. What makes you think you have the right to speak to me or anyone in that harsh, demanding manner?"

He was stunned and embarrassed, realizing that nothing gave him that right. He told me that he has spent the last twenty years trying to live up to what he learned that day—remembering that everyone deserves to be treated with respect, even if he is justifiably angry or disappointed. It was interesting to speak to this man because I was certain that he really had learned something that day, in of all places—a car wash! It was difficult to imagine that this person had ever been rude or insensitive to another human being. He was gentle, sincere, kind, and centered, a real pleasure to be around and, incidentally, one of the top people in his field.

When I observe others who are rude, demanding, or insensitive to a flight attendant, a stranger, waitress, grocery clerk, or whomever, I often ask myself the same question that the car wash manager asked the man in my story: "What gives this person the right to speak like this?" I still don't know the answer to this question—do you? Sometimes people believe that if someone is doing his job, he ought to put up with snobby customers or an arrogant boss. It's always seemed to me, however, that if someone is doing his job, and I'm one of the beneficiaries of their performance, that's all the more reason to speak to him with gratitude and respect. But even beyond what's right and wrong, it's just smart business to speak to others with love and respect.

If you're looking for ways to make your life less stressful, this is one of the keys.

93.

DON'T GO THERE

This is one of my favorite popular expressions. I have no idea where it came from, but I believe that it has some very important implications for all of us. It certainly does for me.

"Don't go there" is an expression that essentially means you know that if you continue on a certain path—thinking in a certain way, arguing, inquiring, discussing, behaving, or whatever—it's going to lead to a predictable, negative result, guaranteed. So, very simply, don't do it! Stop. Don't continue.

For example, you might be asking someone at work a series of personal questions and notice that he is getting increasingly defensive and angry. If there is no actual reason you need the answers to your questions, this might qualify for the "don't go there" wisdom. To continue with your questions virtually guarantees that you will create problems for yourself now or down the road. You'll have a new enemy, or at least someone who is mad at you. Why continue? The same idea applies to so many interpersonal issues. Often, we know deep down what's going to happen if we say certain things to certain people. Sometimes it's best to just "not go there."

Suppose you're feeling sorry for yourself and completely overwhelmed. You're thinking about quitting your job and about how horrible your life has become. Here, the "don't go there" expression would mean "stop thinking along these lines." To continue only guarantees that you're going to feel even worse. What's the point? Wouldn't it be wiser to wait until later, when you feel better, to analyze your life? Why go on when you know the result is going to be pain?

I once had a friend who was about to have an affair. He asked me what I thought. My exact words to him were, "Don't go there." For whatever reason, he didn't, and he and his wife were able to improve their marriage.

For some reason, the simplicity of this expression carries a great deal of power. It's so straightforward that it's capable of stopping you in your tracks, or at least helping you to see the futility of certain thoughts or acts. It can provide the necessary wisdom and perspective to change direction or avoid certain mistakes. So, when you say it to yourself, or when someone says it to you, you're able to take the advice seriously.

I've witnessed many instances where this simple idea could have saved a person's job, prevented an argument, or a great deal of unnecessary stress. Suppose someone is angry at his boss and decides to tell him off while he is still angry. A good friend could have said, "Don't go there." He may have thought twice. Or one of those ridiculous "I'm determined to be right" arguments is just getting started. This same advice could have provided the wisdom to simply allow the other person to be right, thereby saving the trouble and stress of the argument, and leaving time for a peaceful lunch. So often, going down a negative path leads to a series of stressful and destructive actions. If you can nip the problem in the bud early by using these simple words, you can prevent a great deal of stress.

I'd be willing to bet that you can think of many applications of this expression in your life. There are many instances where as simplistic as it may seem, "not going there" is really solid advice.

94.

REMEMBER TO APPRECIATE
THE PEOPLE YOU WORK WITH

One of the most consistent complaints of working people in virtually all industries is that they either feel completely unappreciated, or at the very least under-appreciated. There seems to be an unspoken assumption that workers are lucky to have jobs—and the fact that they have jobs is appreciation enough. Any demands, expectations, or even hopes of verbal or behavioral appreciation is often treated as trivial or unnecessary.

The problem is, people need and deserve to feel appreciated. People who feel appreciated are happier, less-stressed, and more loyal than those who feel taken for granted. Overall, they are harder workers and are excellent team players. They quit less often, show up on time, get along with others, exhibit abundant creativity, and strive for excellence. Conversely, people who are (or even feel) unappreciated often feel resentful and lose their enthusiasm for their work. They can become apathetic and lazy. They are easily bothered, and certainly are no fun to be around or work with. Perhaps most of all, people who feel unappreciated have a tendency to sweat the small stuff.

Unfortunately, I can't create a strategy for feeling appreciated, only one for remembering to appreciate. However, I think you'll discover that, in a way, the two are very closely related. In fact, it has been my experience that the more committed I have become to remembering to appreciate those I work with, the better I have felt about myself. And as an added bonus, those I work with seem to appreciate me much more than ever. In this instance, it really does seem that what goes around comes around.

Even if someone is "just doing her job," it's critical that she feels appreciated. My suggestion is to go out of your way to make sure those you work with know that you genuinely appreciate them. Praise often. Dish out compliments. If it's at all possible and appropriate, send a card, e-mail, or handwritten note. Make a phone call or, even better, look the person in the eye and tell them how much you appreciate them. On occasion if you can do it, and again when appropriate, send a small gift or token of your appreciation. Make your appreciation known. Do all of this often.

For example, even if it's the job of the mailroom guy to bring your mail, thank him when he drops it off. Notice his reaction and notice the way it makes you feel too. Thank the person at the copy shop for copying your papers. So what if it's "her job." Likewise, send an occasional card to thank someone you do business with for using your service. It will always come back to you, several times over. And, even if it didn't, it would still be worth it. Make sure your secretary and/or staff is aware that you value their work and their presence in your life. Make a point of thanking them.

Several times a year, I put a thank-you note outside with our normal garbage delivery and, inside the card, I include a small tip for the garbage collector, who does an extraordinary job. Not only does he wave to me on those occasions when he sees me jogging early in the morning, but he's always happy to take extra trash to the dump.

By remembering to appreciate the people you work with, your business relationships will be enhanced and, as importantly, you'll be actively making everyone's day a little brighter—including your own.

When you dish out a dose of appreciation, take note of how you feel. In all likelihood, you'll feel peaceful and satisfied, like you're on target and headed in the right direction. Offering genuine appreciation is quite stress-relieving. It feels good, not only to the person receiving the appreciation, but to the giver as well. It feels good to know that you're helping another person feel acknowledged. It's also nice to know that you're helping that person bring out the best in themselves.

I remember a time when I was having some difficulty with a person I was working with. I felt she wasn't meeting my professional expectations, and the two of us were engaged in what seemed like petty arguments. Then it dawned on me that, in reality, she was really working hard and probably felt taken for granted. I decided to start over and try a new strategy. Instead of continuing to let her know of my dissatisfaction, I started thinking of the things that she was doing right. I listed her strengths, of which there were many, and I wrote her a thank you note. My compliments were genuine and from the heart. About a week later, I received a beautiful thank you note where she also pointed out how easy, for the most part, I was to work with. As an added bonus, I noticed an almost immediate improvement in those areas that I had felt needed work. With almost no effort and certainly no struggle, I had turned our relationship around and we were back on track.

It's important to know that I didn't issue the thank-you note in an attempt to manipulate her. I did so because I realized that she was feeling under-appreciated. And I was right. As soon as she felt appreciated and knew that it was genuine, she was able to move forward.

It's certainly not always the case that you will receive such immediate and positive feedback. I've been involved in many instances where I felt I was doing a good job being appreciative, yet didn't feel any reciprocal efforts coming back. But you know what? It doesn't matter. Regardless of whether you get anything in return, deep down it feels good and it's the right thing to do. The worst that can happen is that you make someone else feel good. I can't think of very many things that feel better than offering genuine appreciation toward those you work with.

95.

DON'T SWEAT YOUR CRITICS

To be honest, if I became upset or immobilized by my critics, I can guarantee you that you wouldn't be reading this book today. The truth is, critics are a fact of life, and criticism is something all of us must face. In fact, the only way to avoid criticism is to live an isolated life where people aren't exposed to your work, personality, or behavior. Sometimes the criticism we receive is valuable, even helpful. Other times, it's utter nonsense. Either way, learning to see criticism as "small stuff" is incredibly useful in our efforts to live a life of reduced stress.

For as long as I can remember, my goal was to spread joy to as many people as possible. I've spent my career trying to help people become more relaxed and patient, to appreciate life, and to sweat the small stuff less often. Yet despite my good intentions and my love for people, I've been criticized for being everything from a Pollyanna, to simplistic, naive, and unrealistic. I've even had a few people accuse me of attempting to harm people with my message of cheer! For as long as I can remember, a certain percentage of people have told me, "You couldn't possibly be that happy," or "Your life must be easier than mine." There's just no way around it. Someone is always going to have an objection to something you are doing.

If you think about it, a landslide political victory would be one where the winner received 60 percent of the vote. That means that even in a convincing win, 40 percent of the people will be wishing the winner had lost!

Realizing this somewhat startling statistic has helped me to keep the criticism directed at me in its proper perspective. No one is important enough, good enough, or well-intentioned enough to escape their share of criticism.

I asked a fellow author who is extremely calm and nonreactive how he handles bad reviews and criticism. He told me, "I always try to see if there is a grain of truth in what is being said. Quite honestly, there often is. In these instances, I try to learn what I can, and then let go of it. Very often my greatest growth comes directly after a dose of criticism. On the other hand, I've learned that if there's nothing to the criticism, it will simply fade away. The worst thing to do is take it personally and become defensive."

Everyone is entitled to their opinion. We will always run into people who have differing points of view and who see life very differently from the way we do. When this becomes okay with you, criticism won't have the same hold on you that it once did. Remember, the same thing that one person loves will irritate someone else. Something you find funny, I might think of as boring, or vice versa. No matter how hard any of us try, no matter how positive our intentions, there will always be someone there to criticize us. Welcome to the human race. When you make the decision to stop sweating your critics, your ego and self-image won't be hurt any more, and your work life will seem a great deal less stressful.

96.

REDUCE YOUR
SELF-INDUCED STRESS

An insightful colleague of mine with a great sense of humor had a terrific idea for a T-shirt. He was going to call it something like "The Shirt to Take Away Your Stress." He was going to offer a 100 percent guarantee that while you were wearing the shirt, you would never feel any stress—other than that which you create from within your own head!

Obviously, his premise was that all of your stress originates from the way that you think, therefore he would never have to return any money. I wouldn't go quite that far, but his point is well taken. To me, if someone breaks into your home and points a gun to your head—that's real stress. Or if your child is sick, you're fired from your job, or there's a fire in your home, or any of thousands of other real-life scenarios occur, there is good reason to feel stressed.

That being said, however, it's clear that a significant percentage of the stress we feel does indeed originate from within us—from the way we think and hold on to things. Most of us use our thinking as ammunition against ourselves many times a day, without even knowing it. We think like victims or we think ourselves into a corner. We blow things out of proportion and make a big deal out of little things. We overanalyze our lives and exaggerate our responsibilities. We sweat the small stuff. We engage in "thought attacks" and mentally rehearse problems, concerns, and outcomes that may or may not manifest themselves. We engage in negative speculation and attach motives to the behavior of others. We live not in the moment, but in anticipation of future moments.

Or we wallow in the past. We fill our minds with angry, overwhelmed, and stressful thoughts, and all the while wonder why we are so unhappy. We have a series of negative, pessimistic thoughts and take them all very seriously. And for the most part, we are completely unaware that we're doing any of this—nor are we aware of how destructive we are being. Instead, our tendency is to blame the world, our circumstances, and other people for the stress that we feel.

Imagine what would happen to the quality of your life if you were to eliminate or even reduce the self-induced portion of your stress. Because so much of our stress and unhappiness comes from the way that we think, you'd be among the happiest people on earth—without changing a single thing in your life. Why not give it a try?

The hardest part of dealing with self-induced stress is to have the humility to admit that it is, indeed, self-induced. It's much easier to say, "I'm stressed because of the way my life is set up" than it is to say, "I'm stressed because of the way I think." Nevertheless, if you insist on validating and reinforcing how difficult your life is, it's going to be very difficult to change the way you feel. Once you see your part, however, you have the power to change.

Once you can admit that, at least to some degree, you are your own worst enemy, the rest is pretty easy. You can begin by paying attention to your own thoughts—and remembering that you are the one thinking them. When a negative or self-defeating thought runs through your mind, you have the capacity to say, "There's another one," or something similar to acknowledge the fact that your thinking is getting in your own way. You can then gently dismiss the negative thought from your mind, not taking it so seriously. In this way, one by one, you can virtually eliminate negativity from your life. Again, the trick is to see that it's *you* doing it to *you*.

The only lasting way to reduce your stress is to break the habit of thinking in self-defeating ways. More specifically, the solution involves taking your own thoughts—particularly the negative ones— a little less seriously. Remember that they are just thoughts, and be willing to pay less attention to or even dismiss those that are bringing you down or getting in your way.

Start by observing your thoughts. Are you practicing optimism and good mental health? Are you keeping your perspective and sense of humor? Or do you allow your thinking to get the best of you? Do you take your thinking too seriously? If so, this is the place to start. Remember, it's far easier to shift your thinking than it is to shift the ways of the world. By reducing your self-induced stress, you'll be making great strides in your efforts to feel more relaxed and calm.

97.

BECOME AWARE OF
THE THOUGHT FACTOR

Becoming aware of "the thought factor" is without question one of the most important ingredients in learning to stop sweating the small stuff at work—and elsewhere. In order to become a calmer, gentler, and less reactive person, it's essential to understand that your experience of life is created from the inside out—not the other way around, as it so often seems.

My good friend and coauthor of *Slowing Down to the Speed of Life,* Joe Bailey, was involved in an interesting experiment designed to demonstrate this critical point. He interviewed dozens of drivers during rush hour traffic who were on a busy freeway on-ramp in Minneapolis.

The assumption is often made that traffic is one of those irritations that everyone resents. It's often included on stress tests designed to quantify how stressed-out you must be. At best, traffic is tolerated; at worst, it's cause for road rage. Joe's goal, however, was to teach people that, in fact, our thinking, not the traffic itself, is ultimately responsible for the feelings that are experienced in traffic. He was trying to show that we do, indeed, have a choice in how we experience traffic and that we are not victims of traffic—or anything else.

The responses to being stuck in horrible traffic were as varied as the types of cars being driven. As you might expect, a certain percentage of drivers were incensed, red-faced, and completely bothered. Some yelled and cursed at Joe and the camera. Others were accepting and relaxed. Some of them used the time to listen to audio tapes or talk on the phone. And believe it or not, a few actually reported that being in traffic was their favorite time of the day—it was the only time they had to be completely alone. In traffic, they could slow down and relax. No one could bother them or ask them to do anything.

Remember, a vast majority of these people had just finished work. All of them were probably tired. They were in the same traffic jam, delayed for the same amount of time. No one was given any advantages—the circumstances were essentially identical for all. So, if the traffic were actually responsible for our negative reactions, then it would logically follow that the traffic would affect everyone in the same way. It doesn't.

This experiment shows us that our experience of life does, in fact, come from our own thinking and perception. If you carefully consider what I'm suggesting here, you'll see some powerful implications. It means that you really do have a choice in how you respond—not only in traffic, but also in all those other situations that are almost always associated with misery and stress.

If you're in a traffic jam, for example, and can admit to yourself and recognize that your inner experience is being dictated by your thinking (not the traffic), it changes the entire nature of your experience. It reminds you that a shift in your thinking can result in a shift in your stress level. Rather than insisting that life accommodate you with fewer demands and hassles, you can learn to stay relatively unaffected and relaxed in spite of it all. I'm not suggesting that it's always going to be easy. It won't. However, you can see that with this knowledge comes hope. Even when you're really frustrated, it reminds you that it's possible to see the situation differently. Without a doubt, you'll get through it easier than before.

There are certain cause-and-effect relationships in life. If you jump off a fifty-story building, for example, you're not going to live. If you put your hand on a burning stove, it's going to hurt. If you put a giant cork at the bottom of a lake, it's going to rise to the surface. These are laws of nature.

Most of us, however, treat everyday events—traffic, hard work, conflict, mistakes, deadlines, being criticized, and so forth—with a similar cause-and-effect relationship. We assume that these events must cause stress and grief in the same way that fire causes a burn. Events like traffic are assumed to cause upset. Being criticized is supposed to make you feel defensive. Making a mistake is going to lower your spirits, and so forth. The reason we make these erroneous assumptions is because we think the traffic or other stressor is causing our stress, while in actuality it does not.

Understanding this concept can open the door to a whole new way of looking at life and the minor irritations and hassles we all must face. We can't often change our immediate circumstances—but we always have the ability to change our thoughts and attitudes. I hope you'll reflect on this strategy and embrace its compelling logic. Becoming aware of the thought factor will change your life.

98.

EASE OFF YOUR EGO

The goal of this book has been to help you become less stressed at work and to assist you in your efforts to stop sweating the small stuff. I can't think of too many factors that contribute more to our stress, anxiety, and frustration than a large ego. Therefore, easing off your ego is one of the most leveraged efforts you can make to reduce the stress at work.

I think of the ego as that part of us that needs to stand out and be special. And while each one of us is certainly special and unique in our own way, our ego has the need to prove this to everyone. The ego is that part of us that brags, exaggerates, criticizes, and judges others (as well as ourselves). The ego is very self-centered, as if it needs to yell out, "Look at me!" Because the ego is so self-preoccupied and selfish, it encourages us to lose our compassion for and interest in others. Its sole commitment is to maintain itself.

In addition to the obvious drawbacks, the ego is an enormous source of stress. Think about how much energy and attentiveness it takes to prove yourself, show off, and defend your actions. Consider how stressful it is to compare yourself to others and to put yourself down. Think about how draining it is to constantly be keeping score of how you're doing and to be overly concerned with what others think about you. I get tired just thinking about it!

Easing off your ego is accomplished by intention. The first step is to have the desire to shrink your ego down to size and to see how destructive and stressful it can be. The rest is easy. All it takes is humility and patience. Begin paying attention to your thoughts and behavior. When you notice yourself in your "proving mode," gently remind yourself to back off. You can say something simple to yourself like, "Whoops, there I go again." Be sure to laugh at and be easy on yourself. Don't make letting go of your ego into yet another contest with yourself. It's not an emergency. Be patient and it will happen.

There is a lot to be gained by easing off your ego. First and foremost, you'll feel as though a huge burden has been lifted. As I mentioned, it takes a great deal of effort to be on guard and in the proving mode. Therefore, you'll have a great deal more energy and will become more lighthearted. In addition, as you ease off your ego, you'll become much more interested in other people. You'll become a better listener and a kinder, more generous person. This will translate into people liking you even more than they already do. As you let go of the need to impress others and simply be yourself, you'll end up getting more positive attention than ever before. You won't need it, but you'll get it.

I hope you'll give this strategy some careful consideration and gentle effort. If each of us can become more humble, sincere and generous, the world will be a much nicer place. And to top it off, none of us will be sweating the small stuff.

99.

REMEMBER,
SMALL STUFF HAPPENS

As we near the end of this book, I felt it would be helpful to remind you of a key point—small stuff happens. In other words, you could memorize this book, practice every strategy faithfully, and become an incredibly peaceful person. Yet despite all that, and no matter who you are, how successful you become, who your contacts are, or anything else, you're still going to have to deal with your share of "small stuff." Guaranteed. It's important to remind yourself of this fact—regularly—because it can be tempting to believe that your new wisdom and insights or a more positive attitude are somehow going to exempt you from the reality of daily hassles. The question isn't whether or not we will have to deal with such issues, but how we will approach them. With practice, the small stuff you will have to deal with won't seem like such a big deal. Instead, it will be seen as "small stuff."

Even to this day, when I get frustrated over the barrage of small stuff that I have to deal with, my dad reminds me of a quote that, perhaps, says it all: "Life is just one thing after another." How true! You get through one hassle, and another one is just around the corner. You resolve a conflict and inadvertently begin another. You solve a problem and, like magic, another one presents itself. One person is delighted at your performance and in pleasing him, you irritate someone else. Your plans fall through, an error is committed, your computer crashes. It's all part of life, and it's not going to change.

There's something incredibly peaceful in recognizing and surrendering to the fact that small stuff does happen, and that the nature of life is that it's full of conflicting choices, demands, desires, and expectations. It has always been that way and always will be. To assume otherwise creates pain and suffering. Once you stop demanding that life be different, however, the nature of the game changes and you regain control over your life. The same things that used to drive you crazy no longer do. What used to cause you grief, you now see with perspective. Rather than wasting your valuable energy banging your head against walls, you remain calm, deal with the issue as best you can, and move forward.

To the best of my knowledge, there is no magic pill that is going to make your experience of work perfect or trouble-free. I'm certain, however, that by enhancing your perspective and becoming a less reactive, calmer person, you can learn to take life in stride while bringing out the best in yourself. I hope this book has been helpful to you in your efforts to lighten up, enhance your perspective, and most of all, to stop sweating the small stuff.

100.

DON'T LIVE FOR RETIREMENT

Knowingly or unknowingly, many people practically live for retirement. They think about how wonderful life will be without the burden of daily work outside the home. Some people go so far as to count the years, months, even days before retirement. It's common for people to postpone joy, contentment, and satisfaction until "later." It's almost as though people are "putting in time" as if they were serving a sentence, patiently waiting for their freedom.

Admittedly, most people don't go quite this far. It's usually a bit more subtle than this. However, a staggering percentage of people expect that life down the road is going to be better than it is today. Frequently, daydreams as well as conversations with coworkers and friends make it clear that the expectation is that "someday" will be better than now—when you're retired, have more money, freedom, wisdom, time to travel, or whatever.

I'm passionate about this topic because it's clear to me that thinking in these "someday life will be better" terms is a guaranteed way to set yourself up for a long and tiring career. Rather than enjoying each day, being open to new challenges and opportunities, sharing your gifts with others, and being willing to learn from and become inspired by your work-related experiences, you choose instead to essentially put your life on hold, to go through the motions, get stuck in a rut, and, to one degree or another, feel sorry for yourself.

It's far better, I believe, to wake up each morning and remind yourself of the old adage, "Today is the first day of the rest of my life." Make the decision to honor your gift of life by giving today your best effort, regardless of what you happen to do for a living. See if you can keep perspective when others may not, inspire another person, or make a contribution, however small, to the life of someone else. Remind yourself that all days were created equal, that today is every bit as important as any future day after retirement.

Another important reason to avoid living for retirement is that doing so increases the likelihood that you'll be disappointed when it arrives. A strange thing happens when we postpone happiness until a later date. It's as though, in the meantime, we're rehearsing how to be unhappy. We become experts. When we tell ourselves we'll be happy later, what we're really saying is that our life isn't good enough right now. We have to wait until our circumstances are different. So we wait and wait. Thousands of times, over the course of many years, we remind ourselves, in the privacy of our own minds, that when things are different—someday down the road—we'll feel satisfied and happy. But for now, we'll have to make do.

Finally, the big day arrives—the first day of retirement. Yippee!

But here's the problem. As you probably know, old habits die hard. If you smoke or stutter, it's difficult to quit. If you're highly critical or defensive, it's hard to change. If you have bad eating and exercise habits, it takes enormous discipline to make a permanent shift. In the vast majority of cases, most people simply can't do it. It's too hard to change.

Why in the world do we assume that our thinking habits are any different? They're not. In fact, in some ways, learning to think differently is the most difficult habit of all to change. All of us have been trapped from time to time by our own thinking. We become accustomed to thinking in a certain way—so much so, we can't see it any other way.

If you spend years and years thinking that life isn't good enough right now—that something else is going to be better—it's ludicrous to believe that in a single moment when retirement becomes reality, you're going to somehow begin to think differently; that somehow life as it is is suddenly going to be good enough. No way. It's not going to happen. Instead, it's predictable that the opposite will happen. Your mind will continue to believe that something else will be better. You have a habit of seeing life this way, and it's not going to stop simply because your external life has shifted.

The way around this problem is to commit to being happy now—to make the absolute best of the job or career you have right now, to see it as an adventure, to be creative and insightful. Make this your habitual way of thinking about your job and of being in the world. Practice this type of healthy, optimistic thinking on a day-to-day, moment-to-moment basis. If you do, then when retirement arrives, whether it's a year from now or twenty years from now, you will know the secret of happiness: that there is no way to happiness; happiness *is* the way. It will be second nature to you.

So, go ahead and look forward to a fantastic retirement. Plan ahead and plan well. But do yourself a great big favor. Don't miss a single day along the way. I will conclude by saying that I hope this book has been helpful to you and that I send you my love, respect, and best wishes.

Treasure yourself,

Richard Carlson